HIDDEN TREASURES

Heaven's Astonishing Help with Your Money Matters

Leslie Householder
Author of "The Jackrabbit Factor: Why You Can"

The interpretations and applications of scriptures and ideas in this book are solely the author's *and, while based on principles universal in nature, do not necessarily represent official beliefs or doctrine of any particular denomination.*

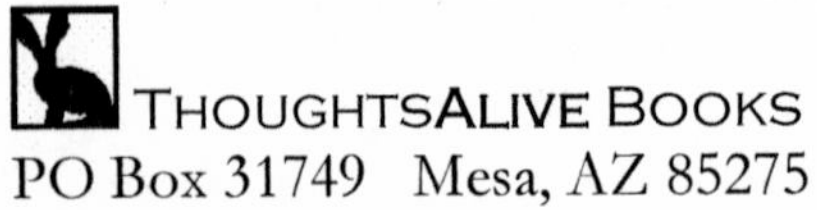

PO Box 31749 Mesa, AZ 85275

First Edition
Printed in the U.S.A.

ISBN 0-9765310-2-X/978-0-9765310-2-9
Library of Congress Control Number: 2005904030

TABLE OF CONTENTS

INTRODUCTION

(Stuff you should know if you want the rest of the book to make sense…)

This book is a sequel to my modern-day allegory, “The Jackrabbit Factor: Why You Can.” While the Jackrabbit story is a fictional introduction to the laws of thought in action, “Hidden Treasures” was intended to answer (in non-fiction format) the question: *Why does it work*? Each book effectively stands alone, although they compliment each other. Together, they help the reader internalize the laws of thought related to prosperity.

While “The Jackrabbit Factor” was designed to be useful to any person who believes in a Higher Power, I get personal in “Hidden Treasures” by touching on some of my personal religious beliefs regarding faith in general which have helped me overcome certain challenges along the way.

I write to those with an uninhibited hunger for understanding. Of course I expect anyone to scrutinize a philosophy and measure it against what feels right to him or her. The references I’ve selected teach principles which I believe will be in harmony with the beliefs of any God-fearing person, no matter what their religious background.

I've written this book out of deep gratitude to God for allowing me to suffer years of financial lack and endure the negative effects of depression. Though I felt abandoned at the time, I can see now that He had everything under control all along. He was causing me to seek and eventually find some powerful answers to some of life's most common questions. Without the experiences that took me through extreme bitterness and despair, I never would have had a reason to search for the answers I'm presenting here. My bitterness has been replaced with gratitude, my despair with hope, my depression with joy, my stress with peace, and the poverty has been replaced with abundance. I'm compelled to share what I've learned because I know I'm not the only one to have ever been frustrated with finances.

Bob Proctor is the man responsible for introducing me to many of the ideas contained in this book. He is a world-renowned speaker, best-selling author, and founder of Life Success Productions. Although he isn't a member of the Church of Jesus Christ of Latter-day Saints, he often quotes a Mormon verse in his seminars. He says, and I agree, that the following one passage beautifully sums up the foundational idea behind the principles of prosperity you will find in this book. The verse reads, "There is a law, irrevocably decreed in heaven before the foundations of this world, upon which all blessings are predicated—and when we obtain any blessing from God, it is by obedience to that law upon which it is predicated" (Doctrine and Covenants 130:20-21).

Note: The interpretation and application of scriptures and ideas here *are my own and do not necessarily represent the beliefs or doctrine of any particular denomination.* You will find the principles contained in this book to be universal.

Most of my life I've tried to live in obedience to God's laws, for I believed that to do so is the only way to true happiness. For quite some time, I believed the best way to be righteous is to live a meager life, so that I would remain forever humble: an attribute necessary for salvation. After all, "a rich man shall hardly enter into the kingdom of heaven" (Matthew 19:23). I believed it was evil to desire riches, and I was certain that the richer a person was, the more miserable they must be, sooner or later.

However, after I married and started a family, I wrestled with a similar dilemma to the one experienced by Adam in the story of Adam and Eve in the Garden of Eden, which I call the "Adam Dichotomy". God gave Adam two commandments: *Don't eat the forbidden fruit,* and *multiply and replenish the earth.* But when Eve partook of the forbidden fruit and was cast out of the garden, Adam had a difficult choice. He could righteously refuse the fruit but fail to replenish the earth, or he could replenish the earth only after following Eve's forbidden action. Either way, he would be ruining a perfect track record.

While I felt guilty coveting the riches of the world (like desiring forbidden fruit), I wanted them simply to help me keep a form of two other commandments: *thou shalt not steal* and *thou shalt not bear false witness.* The way I saw it, if I didn't pay my bills in full and on time, I was not only *robbing* the other party of their just dues, but I had *made a promise* in a contract which I was not keeping. My integrity, or in other words, my *honesty* was on the line.

Furthermore, I now view the Old Testament commandment to "multiply and replenish the earth" in more than one way. To me, it's not *just* a literal directive to have children, but also a symbolic instruction to take whatever I've been blessed with, and multiply it to demonstrate good stewardship. I believe God would have a person strive to multiply what little resources he/she may have, so that he/she can live a more abundant life and serve Him more extensively.

In a sense, then, I partook of the forbidden fruit (sought riches) so that I might multiply my talents and be a better servant of the Lord. After all, I thought about how much more *good* I could do for the Lord if I was not so self-absorbed with *my* needs all the time. I heard it said, “Money isn’t evil; it just makes you more of what you already are. If you’re good, then with money you can do *more* good. If you are evil, then *we don’t want it in your hands*!”

I had finally decided that it was probably okay to “seek riches” against my conscience, rather than resign myself to the smothering prison of debt and the stain of poor credit.

However, obtaining riches was not as easy as I thought it would be. Somehow I believed that if I were just righteous enough, God would prosper me, not just spiritually, but financially as well. I went to church each week. I prayed daily. I donated my time to teaching children and teenagers on Sunday. I fed missionaries who were far from home and needing a meal (even though the meal was never fancy). I babysat for free to give weary mothers (like me) a break. I paid an honest tithing…

...and I suffered from depression. Focusing on the needs of others was *supposed* to bring me joy, but no matter how much I tried to do what was right, I keenly felt the weight of our financial burdens nearly every moment of the day. I felt a growing affinity to the children of Israel who begged for deliverance from their slavery in Egypt. But where was my Moses, sent to deliver *me*?

My husband and I ventured into a few money-making ideas, and we personally kept the self-help industry in business, or so it felt. The way I remember it, we sacrificed anything we could in order to keep our bills paid, and also feed our minds to learn to succeed. I sold my wedding dress and flute at a yard sale. I was so desperate for money that I actually sold my Young Women's Medallion to a *very* excited middle-aged lady. I'm embarrassed to say that I hadn't realized it wasn't just a pendant that could be replaced at my local Deseret Bookstore. (Gratefully, years later when I was asked to fill a position in the Young Women's Organization, my good bishop arranged to provide me with a replacement.)

I also remember traveling across the country to attend a seminar once, with no room on a credit card for the rental car, and a can of corn in our backpack. If we had an opportunity to spend time with a mentor, we took it; even if it had to be at

10:00 p.m., two hours from home. We'd arrange for an overnight sitter (an insomniac member of our congregation), and return in the early morning hours, just in time to clean some office buildings as janitors and then go to work at our regular jobs. We invested in motivational seminars, books, and tapes regularly for about seven years.

Crazy? Yeah, maybe so; but simply put, we were hungry for insight. Through our study, it became clear that our attitude had everything to do with our success, but we still constantly fell back into our old thinking patterns, failing to pull out of our financial bondage. While my husband remained committed to continual growth and learning, I eventually became jaded and weary from years of effort with hardly anything to show for it.

Having decided to quit trying, I nevertheless consented to attend just ONE more seminar, which I determined would be my last. I decided to give up the effort to try to change our lifestyle, and just settle in; grateful for life the way it was, even in all its misery.

I guess the Lord knew what was going on with me, because He sent Bob Proctor to be the guest speaker. It was one of those experiences where I felt, for a moment, that the entire presentation was put together *just for me.* Bob had an amazing message. Part-way through his presentation, my husband and I just looked at each other with our mouths wide open. Unlike many of the other seminars we attended, here was no hype. While enthusiasm is an effective way to get a person going, this one had a different effect on us. His message *required* no hype, because it was just an unbelievably simple but powerful explanation of how the Universe operates.

The real reasons for our financial bondage became absolutely clear, and I realized why God had *not* prospered us, nor *would* He prosper us until we began obeying His laws specifically governing *prosperity*.

I had been hoping for *monetary* blessings by relying on a few *spiritual* laws. I had reduced everything I had been taught down to one simple false philosophy: *be good and you'll prosper*...which is about as absurd as thinking that so long as you obey the speed limit, you can shoplift without consequence. Different laws have different consequences attached. I learned that if I wanted to prosper financially, I had to quit breaking the laws that governed prosperity. For one thing, I hadn't known they existed, and for another thing, I hadn't known I was breaking them.

As I learned the laws governing the abundant life, I gratefully discovered they are in perfect harmony with the commandments I had been raised to follow. I didn't have to face another "Adam Dichotomy," because I would not be required to break any commandments to live by these new-to-me laws of prosperity. In fact, I discovered that to live by them, my ability to live the precepts of my religion was actually enhanced.

Interestingly enough, at the seminar we were surrounded by other individuals, not of our faith, who were just as captivated and strengthened in their own faith as we were. It was enlightening, and unifying.

As you could guess, the first seminar with Bob Proctor wasn't my last seminar after all. We returned about six months later to hear him expound for three more days; and as we consciously began to live in harmony with the laws of prosperity, our monthly income tripled within four more months. By the end of the fourth month, we also had moved to a larger, more beautiful home in a safer neighborhood, turning our previous home into a rental, even though we had previously been going "in the hole" several hundred dollars a month.

The change had been attained so easily, and the difference was so dramatic, that I could hardly sit still. Filled with profound gratitude to God for our newfound knowledge, I *had* to share what I knew. So when Life Success Productions sent out a call for program facilitators, I jumped at the opportunity. The training cost us a small fortune, but by this time we had accumulated just that much in savings. For once we were able to invest in ourselves on a cash basis. The training was mind-blowing, and living by the principles began to come more naturally with practice. As a result, I've been able to develop a quiet confidence in the Lord that He will always provide for my needs. I've found my wings and developed a unique way of bringing this information to my niche audience outside of my association with Life Success Productions.

Bottom line: I had always been taught over and over not to fear and to trust God; but until I had a working knowledge of His laws connected with the blessing of prosperity, I didn't know how to have that kind of faith.

Soon after becoming a program facilitator, I stumbled onto SheLovesGod.com and responded to an article written by the founder, Marnie Pehrson. That began a conversation which eventually led me to share what I had learned with her. Marnie says, *"As a direct result of learning these laws, I've tripled my internet income, and my husband has retired from his day job to start his own personal chef business (which he's been dreaming about for years)! To say the information is life changing would be an understatement."* ~ Marnie Pehrson, author of "Waltzing with the Light," "Back in Emily's Arms," and founder of SheLovesGod.com and IdeaMarketers.com. In 2002, and at her request, I wrote a series of articles about these laws for her subscribers, which eventually turned into an Ecourse under the title, "Heavenly Help with Money Matters," which is still available online at ThoughtsAlive.com. Over time, that collection of articles was compiled and revised to become the book you hold in your hands.

For more than a year, I presented the principles on the internet with exclusive reference to the King James Version of the Bible, and just a few secular works as well that supported the ideas. I saw an opportunity to take what I had learned from Bob Proctor, and bring it specifically to the Christian audience. Since his ideas were completely in harmony with my own religious beliefs, it was an easy thing to put them in a spiritual context. Since then, I have found other references from Mormon literature which offer additional "witness" for the prospective legitimacy of these principles.

My first idea for the book was to gather *all* supporting literature from *all* major religions of the world for a landmark project that could improve the lives of all God-fearing people across the globe. The wider the market, the better, I was told. But in a way, that's what Bob is already doing. Besides, I realized there is *so* much written about it, it would have been insane to try to pull off my original idea. In fact, the world is so filled with this wisdom taught from so many angles that it is a wonder how I had been blind to it before. The principles governing prosperity may be some of the most fundamental doctrines to be shared by all major religious sects. After all, truth is truth, and truth seekers will cling to truth no matter where they find it. As a member of the Church of Jesus Christ of Latter-day Saints (a Mormon), I saw a pressing need among my friends and family to take these ideas and bring them together from my personal point of view. I was simply a mother of young children who wanted to stay home and raise her family, and who successfully applied the laws of thought to achieve a few of her objectives.

Note: you do not have to embrace my religion to see the principles of prosperity work for you. Simply put, God's power permeates the Universe and as we live in harmony with His laws connected to prosperity, we are blessed with the miracles of the abundant life. In fact, many people of all religions live in harmony with these laws *unknowingly* and thus prosper, not even understanding the real reason why.

Anyway, the following information seems true to me. It has borne good fruit in my life and I'm pleased to share a few of the good seeds with you now. I invite you to bring your faith, great or small, and let me see if I can help increase it. After you read this book, go ahead and ask God in your own way whether or not the ideas presented meet His approval for your life. If you feel peace and joy, then you can know it is good. If you feel confusion and uncertainty, then trust whatever alternative guidance He provides. That process works for me, and has yet to steer me wrong. Reason it out, draw your own conclusion, and then ask if your conclusion is accurate.

> "But, behold, I say unto you, that you must study it out in your mind; then you must ask me if it be right, and if it is right I will cause that your bosom shall burn within you; therefore, you shall feel that it is right. But if it be not right you shall have no such feeling, but you shall have a stupor of thought that shall cause you to forget the thing which is wrong" (Doctrine &Covenants 9:8-9).

I just hope that you'll find within these pages a wider panoramic view of how the Universe seems to operate, a perspective that leaves you feeling enlightened, empowered, and more faithful than ever. This is what it's done for me. So, with mutual respect for our beliefs, whatever they may be, let's proceed...from here on I'll speak to you freely about the things I've discovered.

A FEW BASIC QUESTIONS

I've learned on a personal level the truth in the promise that "He that diligently seeketh shall find; and the mysteries of God shall be unfolded unto them, by the power of the Holy Ghost, as well in these times as in times of old, and as well in times of old as in times to come" (1 Nephi 10:19, *Book of Mormon*).

Life's experiences can often seem random, leading us to ask some pretty serious questions. Yet, I've also learned that for every question there is an answer, and there are few promises in the scriptures that are repeated as often as the promise that if we seek, we shall find; and if we ask, we shall receive. I hope that this work will serve to bring you answers to the questions you might be seeking now. Some of these questions may include:

- *Does God want me to be poor? Does He want me to have plenty of money? Or, does it even matter to Him?*
- *Where will the money come from?*

- *How is it that I'm telling God, "No thank you" right now to the blessings of abundance that He has available to me?*
- *What unseen things are happening for my benefit when I choose to express gratitude to God?*
- *What role does God play in my financial life?*
- *What can I do RIGHT NOW to make a difference RIGHT NOW?*
- *How is my stress and fear reinforcing the unfavorable circumstances in my life?*
- *What unseen things are happening when I feel fear and how does knowing what is happening serve to conquer the fear?*
- *What one idea can I learn that will give me the power to apply faith with confidence?*
- *How can I change my faith into a sure knowledge that my needs will most definitely be met?*

God hasn't told us we're *supposed to* seek riches, but He has told us that if we seek, we will find. Do you believe that? Do you think that each time (and there *are* quite a few times) He said in the Bible, "Seek and ye shall find," He was only talking about salvation? When He said, "Ask and it shall be given you," was He only talking about Living Water? No, I personally don't think so. Whatever worthy thing we need, *that* is what He will provide, *if we ask*. You'll learn in this book how to do just that.

Perhaps He hasn't *commanded* us to seek riches per se; however, many have felt His nudgings to get out of debt, live within our means, build or support the kingdom of God, serve missions, or to simply maintain our properties that we may be wise and faithful stewards of the blessings He has already given us. We know we should feed the poor and bring relief to the needy. I'm certain that He also wants us to raise our families in a responsible way... providing ample nourishment, education, and developing strong relationships which require quality time spent together.

Some are compelled to use their resources to search out their heritage, thus further strengthening their family bonds. Others feel compelled to be self-reliant and prepared for emergencies with a supply of food and fuel, or have at least a few months income saved in case of a job loss or downturn in the economy. Others have a burning desire to get an education of their own to help them reach their God-given potential.

Every faithful, God-fearing human being is compelled to *do something*. In many cases, that *something* requires a little bit of "lucre" just to get it done.

Quite frankly, we need more money than *just enough* for scraping by each month. If we feel God has asked certain things of us, then we can know he has prepared a way for us to accomplish them. As an ancient leader (circa 600 B.C.) named Nephi said,

> "I will go and do the things which the Lord hath commanded, for I know that the Lord giveth no commandments unto the children of men, save he shall prepare a way for them that they may accomplish the thing which he commandeth them" (1 Nephi 3:7, *Book of Mormon*).

God would not compel us to do this or that without preparing a way for us to make it happen. It would be ludicrous to think He would tell us to do something and then sit back and leave us stuck with an impossible task. He doesn't always make it easy, and the answers to our dilemmas are not always obvious, because through our search and struggle we grow. He is more interested in our personal growth than He is in our comfort...and if we can step outside of our troubles long enough to see the implications of that idea, we will realize that His parenting techniques aren't all that bad. We can learn to trust Him.

We can trust that He will help us grow in self-reliance through our struggles. When we are able to care for our own needs, we are more inclined to search outside of our lives to help someone else. Marion G. Romney, former First Counselor in the First Presidency of the Church of Jesus Christ of Latter-day Saints said,

> "Without self-reliance one cannot exercise these innate desires to serve. How can we give if there is nothing there? Food for the hungry cannot come from empty shelves. Money to assist the needy cannot come from an empty purse…
>
> "There is an interdependence between those who have and those who have not. The process of giving exalts the poor and humbles the rich. In the process, both are sanctified. The poor, released from the bondage and limitations of poverty, are enabled as free men to rise to their full potential, both temporally and spiritually. The rich, by imparting of their surplus, participate in the eternal principle of giving. Once a person has been made whole, or self-reliant, he reaches

> out to aid others, and the cycle repeats itself" (Romney, Marion G. "The Celestial Nature of Self-Reliance," *Ensign,* June 1984, 3).

Everyone is somewhere in the middle of this cycle. Are we rich, needing to show humility through giving, or are we poor, learning the hard lessons of how to graciously receive? Hopefully we are not the kind of rich person who hoards his/her blessings; and hopefully we're not the kind of poor person who takes unfair advantage of other people's charity. In every position along the cycle, we have the choice of what kind of attitude we will foster. In any case, the following scripture outlines the order our priorities must follow, if we want to live in harmony with God's will for us:

> "But before ye seek for riches, seek ye for the kingdom of God. And after ye have obtained a hope in Christ ye shall obtain riches, if ye seek them; and ye will seek them for the intent to do good—to clothe the naked, and to feed the hungry, and to liberate the captive, and administer relief to the sick and the afflicted" (Jacob 2:18-19, *Book of Mormon*).

I'll add here that we will do all these things for our *own* families too. We will care for our own, and liberate ourselves from financial captivity, and administer relief to ourselves if we are sick with financial worry.

So, would you like a few Hidden Treasures? Could you use a little bit of Heaven's Astonishing Help with your Money Matters? It matters. It matters that you rely on God for the help you need. We could do everything right, find wealth, and then fail to give Him the credit for our deliverance, however:

> "In nothing doth man offend God, or against none is his wrath kindled, save those who confess not his hand in all things" (Doctrine and Covenants 59:21).

Once we *are* finally delivered, we need to recognize the Source of our deliverance, and follow the advice:

> "If riches increase, set not your heart upon them" (Psalms 62:10).

If God really wants me to be wealthy, why hasn't He already made me so? Again, I believe the reason is because He is more interested in our personal growth than our comfort. The struggle is part of the blessing, believe it or not. To prosper without the struggle is to never comprehend the *value* of the gift of deliverance. Furthermore, struggles keep us going to our knees... and *anything that does* that is a blessing in disguise.

> "And if men come unto me I will show unto them their weakness. I give unto men weakness that they may be humble; and my grace is sufficient for all men that humble themselves before me; for if they humble themselves before me, and have faith in me, then will I make weak things become strong unto them" (Ether 12:27, *Book of Mormon*).

Even our ability to meet financial obligations can become one such strength.

He allows us to suffer financial stress and worry in hopes that we will turn to Him for answers. When we do, He provides those answers. Sometimes He waits until we are sufficiently humble to appreciate the answers. If I had been given these answers too soon, I would not have felt so strongly about sharing my answers with you. In fact, I wouldn't have appreciated them. I might not have even believed them.

Earlier in my life, I tried to be ultra-obedient...to a fault. I realize now that all those years, I was trying to *perfect myself.* Eventually I caved, because it is literally impossible to become perfect on our own. I hadn't yet learned how to rely on a Savior to make up the difference for my deficiencies.

Ironically, the answers to my *financial* dilemmas came after I finally gave up trying. I had gone emotionally limp, and told God that if He wanted me to get out of bed the next morning, He would have to be the one responsible for it. Just about all I could commit to was to pray every morning and night for the following two weeks. No extra-curricular service projects, no promises to be a perfect mother, no guarantee of anything but a humble heart and a commitment to pray often. I had given up trying to be perfect, and told Him apologetically that this was all I could promise right now.

No longer did I feel angry at myself for my failings, I simply was in the depths of sadness that I had finally realized how hopeless I was, and how I wasn't able to be perfect, no matter how hard I tried. I had believed that if I was just disciplined enough, or strong enough, I could have been that 'super-woman'. But no; now I knew it would remain beyond my reach no matter how good I tried to be. I lamented my defeat, and let go of any hope I had that I could ever live the perfect life.

Paradoxically, for the first time in years and at that moment, I finally felt Him smiling on me. It is as if He was saying, "You finally realize your dependence on me, NOW we can proceed!"

Since then, I've learned that I accomplish more and do greater things when I maintain that attitude of humility and acknowledge that if I ever accomplish anything noteworthy, it is because God made it happen through me, and in spite of me. It is through His Spirit that I can wake each morning and believe that the day is worth getting up for. It is because of that experience and many since that I've learned I am truly nothing without Him, and can do no good thing on my own. But I didn't learn this valuable lesson until I gave it my all for as long as I could, and found that I still came short.

So where are you at? Do you feel you've given it your all and you're ready to let God step in and help you achieve success His way? How teachable are you *right now*?

In case you skipped the Introduction (let's be honest...I know some people just want to get right down to business), I need to emphasize again that the interpretation and application of scriptures and ideas here are *my own* and *do not necessarily represent the beliefs or doctrine of any particular denomination.* Alrighty? Then let's go!

ALL ABOUT LAWS

Have you ever violated a man-made law? Say, for example, a traffic law?

How many times *have* you violated a traffic law?

How many times have you been *caught*?

Do those figures match? Of course they don't. When we talk about *law*, it is natural to immediately think of the kind of laws with which we are most familiar. In our everyday life, we are more likely to chat with our spouse or a friend about the guy who cut us off to make an illegal lane change or the new tax bracket for which we just qualified. These are kind of mushy laws, though. What do I mean by that? I mean that these laws are *supposed* to be strictly observed, but when they are not, sometimes the violator suffers a civil consequence; sometimes it seems to go unpunished.

So when someone tries to tell you that there are natural laws governing prosperity, or success, there is a tendency to think, "I wouldn't bank on it." "It may be true, but I wouldn't count on it working in *every* case." Or, "Sounds like a 'get rich quick' scheme. They're only after my money." Or, "There's no such thing as '*one formula* fits all' to making money."

Let me explain something...when you think of law, don't think of man-made laws. They're just not absolute enough to compare with the ideas I'll be presenting here. When I say "law," rather think of something like *gravity*. Gravity is a natural law (a law of nature) that is dependable and constant. You don't have to believe in it; you don't have to like it. In fact, you don't even have to understand it. But you *are* still subject to it. Everything is subject to it. When we seem to "defy" it, it is because we are using other laws which are dependable and constant as well. We can use our knowledge of laws to our advantage. Ignorance of the laws leaves us limited in our abilities.

One thing I like to point out at this stage of the game is the following idea. With reference to the fact that you don't have to believe in a law to be subject to it, picture this: Suppose that you have firm belief in "mind over matter." You choose not to believe in the law of gravity. You decide that you don't want to be subject to it *any more*. So you go to the edge of a cliff, and with all of the positive thinking you can muster, you step off. It's no surprise that, once again, gravity proves true and your "mind over matter" turns into a "mind all~a~smatter."

"Mind over matter" is a true principle, don't get me wrong. But it only works when we apply it in harmony with *natural laws*. Remember *that* as you read on; because, if you find that you're having a hard time believing any of the laws that I'll present, so be it. Just remember that it'll save you from a lot of pain if you choose to believe them anyway.

More about 'Law': I think man-made laws such as traffic laws should rather be called "traffic codes of conduct." Tax laws should be called "tax rules." We need them, but they aren't as dependable as the term "law" would indicate. For the sake of this book, it's important that when I say *law*, I'm talking about something absolute, something unbreakable, and something that just "is." You cannot *break* a law; you can only *break yourself against it*. If you violate the law, you will most definitely be sorry you did, and unfortunately there is no mercy if you're ignorant. The consequences will come, regardless of your understanding of the law.

Spiritual laws can be conditional. Sin is when you transgress a spiritual law after you have been given the law and are capable of understanding it. Let me explain:

Suppose a one year-old child snatches a toy from his three year-old brother. The spiritual law, had he completely understood it would have instructed him "thou shalt not steal." If he knew better and did it anyway, that would have been sin. Of course, a one year-old child is incapable of understanding such a principle, so he is innocent. John 9:41 says,

> "Jesus said unto them, If ye were blind, ye should have no sin: but now ye say, We see; therefore your sin remaineth."

In other words, your innocence is directly related to the degree with which you understood the law.

Think again about the baby. He doesn't understand the spiritual law, so he will not suffer any eternal consequences typically attached to violation of that spiritual law. However, the *natural law* of Cause and Effect is an absolute law. No allowance is made for ignorance. The baby stealing the toy from his brother will discover the effects of this law when his older brother begins screaming and crying and perhaps even inflicting pain on the poor little baby!

Understand that God did *not* apply the consequence. The consequence was spontaneous and natural. I believe that God would prefer his children suffer no pain, but we live in a natural world that is governed by natural laws. Natural laws are laws that even God will not alter. He does not control the outcome of our abiding or violating them. He does, however, understand them perfectly, and tries to teach us through the scriptures and His prophets how to live in harmony with them so that perhaps by our obedience we may avoid painful, natural consequences.

The beautiful thing about understanding the laws is that if we choose to live in harmony with them, we will also be following God's spiritual laws because they are in harmony with each other. We will find that we can enjoy happiness, peace, and abundance now, and eternal joy in the hereafter. What more could God want for His children?

> "There is a law, irrevocably decreed in heaven before the foundations of this world, upon which all blessings are predicated— And when we obtain any blessing from God, it is by obedience to that law upon which it is predicated" (Doctrine and Covenants 130:20-21).

There are laws attached to good health, to loving relationships, and yes, even to wealth.

Are we supposed to be poor? What about Matthew 19:24?

> "It is easier for a camel to go through the eye of a needle, than for a rich man to enter into the kingdom of God."

How do we deal with *that* concept? We look at the context in which it was probably written. I've heard it said that in the days of Jesus, the eye of a needle represented an entryway to a city. It was small enough for a camel to enter, *only* if the camel crawled through on its knees. This is symbolic of humility, and a willingness to remove all extra baggage so that we may squeeze through.

So, if we want to live prosperously, AND we want to still 'go to heaven', we must be certain that our heart is in the right place: would we be able to give it all up? Can we remain full of gratitude and maintain humility in spite of our prosperity? We're warned that it is a hard thing to do. But what is the alternative? Is it better to remain needy or could we do a lot of good for His sake if God showed us how to prosper? Consider this:

Satan would have us believe that we are better off poor. Why? Because if all God-fearing people are broke and needy, and all the unscrupulous people are wealthy, who will run the media? Who will become the political leaders? Who will make the movies and design the fashions of the day? Who will have the greatest influence on society? Fellow principled people...we *need* abundance! *Fear not* to prosper! Increase your devotion and hold fast to righteous principles... but let Him prosper you!

The 'Competitive' Versus the 'Creative' Plane

Whenever riches are obtained in an "unlawful" manner, specifically, in violation of natural laws, the prosperity is temporary. For example, many get rich on a *competitive plane*. Let me explain: picture a pie, with one piece which belongs to you. If your piece of the pie represents the prosperity or wealth you enjoy, then to get more, someone must get less, (see fig. 1 and fig. 2).

On the other hand, you will see that to obtain wealth on a *creative* plane, you are adding some pie to the outer rim of your piece, increasing the diameter of the pie; and because *Nature Abhors a Vacuum,* the rest of the pie gets filled in, by law, and a bigger pie is created for everyone, (fig. 3 and fig. 4). This is in harmony with natural law, and spiritual law. You will learn more about the Vacuum Law of Prosperity in the Bonus section near the end of this book.

Operating on the Competitive Plane

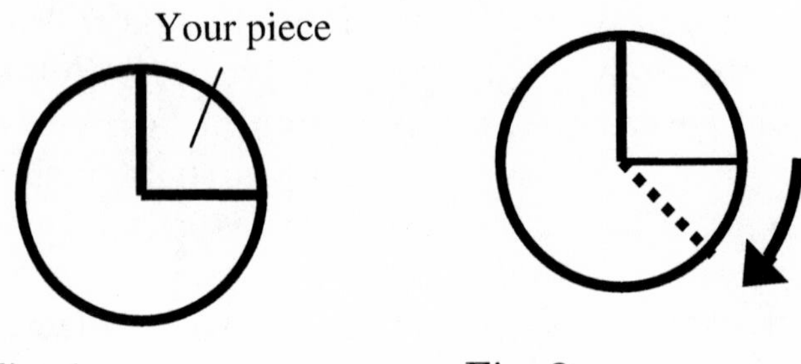

Fig. 1 Fig. 2

(For yours to get bigger, someone else's must get smaller)

Operating on the Creative Plane

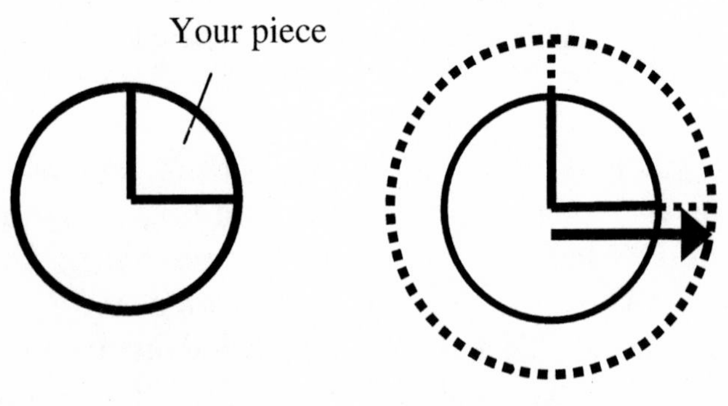

Fig. 3 Fig. 4

As you creatively make yours bigger, the pie grows larger for everyone!

How does it work? Here's an example. At one time I decided to conduct my first workshop to teach these principles. It began with a simple idea. As I continued in that thought, I was led to reserve a conference room at a local hotel. I ordered refreshments. I provided materials. I used gasoline in my car. I hired a babysitter. I picked up presentation materials at the local office supply store, and on the day of the presentation, when we paused for a lunch break, I ate out with my husband.

I was compensated for conducting the workshop. Did I compete with anyone for the revenue? No. Did I increase the size of the pie for anyone else? Well, let's see. Let me list some of the people who benefited financially from my effort:

Hotel owner
Caterer
Materials producer
Gas station owner
Babysitter
Restaurant owner

...and even the *participants* came away filled to overflowing with information and skills to give them the power to prosper. Win, win, win, win, win, win, and win...all the way around! There are no losers. As if the prosperity materialized out of thin air, we all came away from the experience just a little wealthier. I'd like to think the Lord did the happy dance that day.

We can learn to be creative, and live in peace knowing that our needs can be met without diminishing anyone else's portion. This is in harmony with God's Universal Laws.

So, ultimate success = happiness and abundance here and now, and eternal life and exaltation in the hereafter. It is a worthy thing to desire, and you can have it.

While we are promised in Mathew 7:7, "Ask, and it shall be given you," the problem is we don't *really* believe it. That's right, we don't. How often do you kneel in prayer, petitioning the Lord for a certain thing, *knowing* He's going to give it to you just because you asked? Why is it so hard to believe? Because we don't know that there are absolute laws we can *depend* on. If you lack faith in God, then you can trust the laws and your faith in God will be strengthened. Isn't that wonderful?!

If your faith in God is already immovable, then gaining an understanding of the laws will come easy. If you are accustomed to trusting in His laws, then *more* laws will not seem restrictive, but actually liberating. How could that be? Think of the laws like a kite string. It is the *string* that enables the kite to soar! Even though it seems that the string is *preventing* the kite from reaching greater freedoms, *without* the string the kite will fall to the ground. (This analogy was derived from a story told by Patricia P. Pinegar in "Peace, Hope, and Direction," Ensign, Nov. 1999, 67.) So, celebrate that we are given laws; be grateful that He wants to enlighten our minds to understand them.

> "Law, not confusion, is the dominating principle in the universe... This being so, man has but to right himself to find that the universe is right. And during the process of putting himself right, he will find that as he alters his thoughts towards things and other people, things and other people will alter towards him" (Allen, James. *As a Man Thinketh.* New York: Peter Pauper Press, Inc., p. 27).

Even with little apparent rhyme or reason to our circumstances, we are empowered when we understand the laws. In fact, when we pass on to the other side, I believe we will discover that life *was* fair. We just didn't understand all of the universal laws governing us. James Allen was a writer at the turn of the twentieth century, whose essay on the subject is now gaining wider acclaim than ever. A few of his most profound comments solidify these principles, causing the ideas to seem like plain old common sense. In his words:

> "When he begins to reflect upon his condition and search diligently for the law upon which his being is established, [a man] then becomes the wise master, directing his energies with intelligence and fashioning his thoughts to fruitful issues. Such is the conscious master, and man can only thus become by discovering within himself the laws of thought" (Allen, p. 10).

> "That he is the maker of his character, the molder of his life, and the builder of his destiny, [a man] may unerringly prove, if he will watch, control, and alter his thoughts, tracing their effect upon others and his life and circumstances, linking cause and effect by patient practice and investigation" (Allen, 11).

> "Every man is where he is by the law of his being; the thoughts which he has built into his character have brought him there, and in the arrangement of his life there is no

> element of chance, but all is the result of a law which cannot err. This is just as true of those who feel 'out of harmony' with their surroundings as of those who are contented with them" (Allen, 14).

Just as true… even if you feel 'out of harmony' with your surroundings. In other words, you may think you hate your circumstances, but on a subconscious level, you feel right at home. You must change what is happening in your mind, consciously and subconsciously, so that your surroundings will begin to reflect the life you *want,* instead of the life you have. How? Read on…

So what are some of these "laws of our being," anyway? This book will discuss the following seven laws. These are the names by which I learned them. Although I have seen them called different things, these are the terms I will use:

The Law of Perpetual Transmutation
The Law of Relativity
The Law of Vibration
The Law of Polarity
The Law of Rhythm
The Law of Cause and Effect
The Law of Gender/Gestation

While I learned these ideas from Bob Proctor, founder of Life Success Productions, he will be the first to tell you that they weren't his original ideas either. Having been (I believe) a VP of Sales for the Nightingale-Conant Corporation many years ago, he drew from his thirty years of study and reduced the best of the best ideas to their simplest and most precise form. Following is my own personal religious angle on a few of his philosophies.

You'll want to think of these laws as tools in your "toolbox." Every situation you face throughout your life can be dealt with successfully by reaching into your toolbox and selecting the right law on which to focus at the time. This is how engineers and inventors operate: they know the laws of physics. If they want a massive hunk of metal to sail through the air for thousands of miles without falling, they don't have a panic attack about the law of gravity; rather, they respectfully set it aside and instead focus their attention on the laws of aerodynamics. For many, many years, the human race was completely unaware of the laws governing air travel. The laws were always there, and always available for our benefit. But until our awareness was heightened to understand the laws, we were grounded, so to speak.

You'll discover there's no reason to get all crazy when something in your life seems to be falling apart, you'll simply run down your list of laws and focus on the one that keeps your massive hunk of metal sailing through the air, if you will. You'll think on the laws that keep you faithful and productive at the time.

Scientists employ trajectory laws and the law of gravity, (keeping them in perfect balance) in order to keep a satellite in orbit, but disregard laws related to friction because they are simply irrelevant to the task at hand. It would be a waste of energy to be concerned about how much friction will be present upon re-entry if they *never* intend to bring it back to earth. By the same token, when we are experiencing a certain challenge, it is up to us to think only of the laws that help us at the time. We must not get worked up about other laws that have no practical application to our problem. I think you'll know what I mean as we get into the laws more deeply.

Now, if you're up for some fun, take a moment here to play a little interactive game, which you may have seen before. It will be your job to find all numbers, 1-60 in sequential order on the screen. Turn on your computer and go to:

http://www.thoughtsalive.com/tests/numbersearch1.html

When you're done, return to this page.

Welcome back! Do you see how useful an understanding of laws can be? Good! (Don't worry, if you didn't get to play the game, you'll still get the point by reading the book.) Now, I'm here to let you know that there are even *more* laws that govern *other* mysteries. Becoming aware of them is the first liberating step to freedom. It really isn't all that complicated. In fact, it's so simple that many people have disregarded the ideas as *too* simple to be of any significance.

Oh, how familiar *that* scenario is! Take a moment to remember the story from Exodus of Moses and the brass serpent:

> "And the Lord sent fiery serpents among the people, and they bit the people; and much people of Israel died...And the Lord said unto Moses, Make thee a fiery serpent, and set it upon a pole: and it shall come to pass, that every one that is bitten, when he looketh upon it, shall live" (Numbers 21:6, 8).

All they had to do was look, but many people died because they thought the remedy was too simple. So it is with the principles of prosperity. They are simple, but powerful enough to 'save you' in many ways.

The goal is to keep your thoughts where they need to be, for your thoughts shape your circumstances. Your heightened awareness of these laws alone will make a significant difference in the way you think, and the effects of a heightened awareness will be felt even before you finish reading this book.

Hidden Treasures does not claim to teach everything there is to know on the subject. Nevertheless it should be sufficient information to help you make some significant changes in your life. As you learn and apply your knowledge of these laws, you'll find greater joy in your struggles, have deeper faith in God and His promises, and feel a greater measure of peace in what the future has in store for you.

LESSON 1:

LAW OF PERPETUAL TRANSMUTATION

That's just a fancy way of saying that everything is either coming into physical form or going out of it.

Take water, for example. Water can go from invisible humidity or vapor in the air, to visible clouds, to tangible rain, to something even as solid as ice. At any point during the water's transformation, the process can reverse. A cloud does not necessarily turn to rain. Sometimes it disappears again into the clear blue sky. Rainfall doesn't always turn to ice; sometimes it simply evaporates again and disappears into the air, (fig. 5).

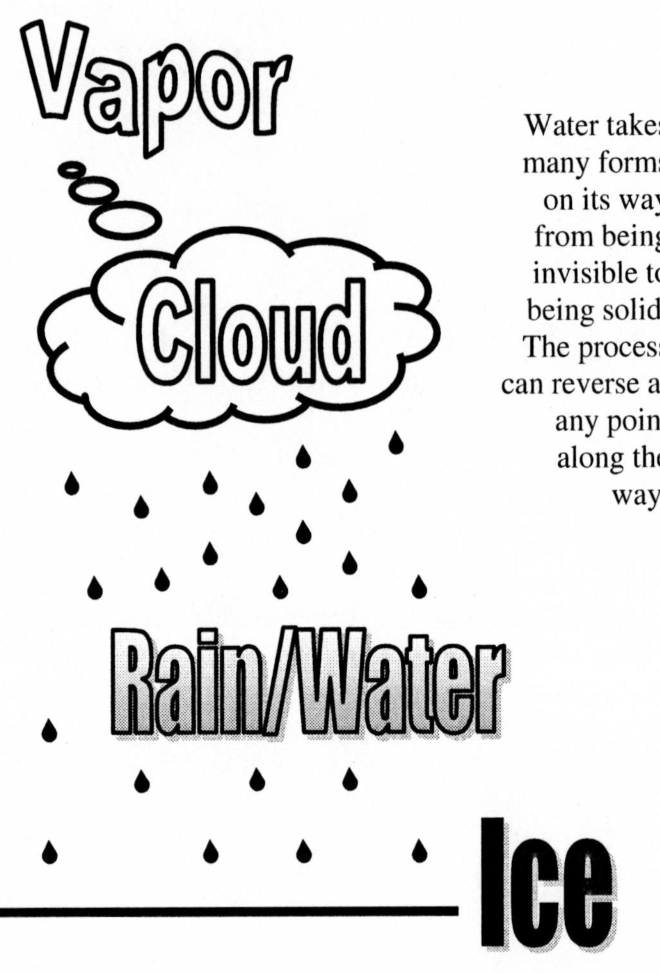

Water takes many forms on its way from being invisible to being solid. The process can reverse at any point along the way.

Fig. 5

So now think about an idea of prosperity. Perhaps for you, prosperity would mean more family time. A family picture as you are posed in front of the Egyptian Pyramids could represent your idea of prosperity. You see yourself and your family members with you, huddled together, smiling, with the pyramids in the background. Now put yourself in the picture, and see the photographer taking it. You feel the sun beating down on you, and the dust blowing by in the mild, whistling breeze. There is laughter from your child or grandchild. You hear the photographer tell your group to hold still and say, “Mummy!” And then you can picture the group disassembling, and walking back to the tour bus. Or camel. Are you thirsty? What would you like?

This situation may be compared to the changing forms of water. The situation has not manifested itself in the physical world yet (just as vapor is not yet rain), but for a moment, the circumstances required to make that situation a reality were actually beginning to gather, as a cloud gathers in the sky. If you were to hold on to that idea, and not throw it out with disbelief or apathy, then eventually, it would happen in real life. Belief keeps the “idea cloud” gathering until it is so heavy that the rain must begin to fall: the circumstances you need *begin to present themselves.* Just like water that can change from an invisible to visible state, so can the Egyptian vacation idea transmute itself into reality. However, disbelief and apathy will, by law, cause the cloud of your idea to dissipate back into the clear blue sky, (fig. 6).

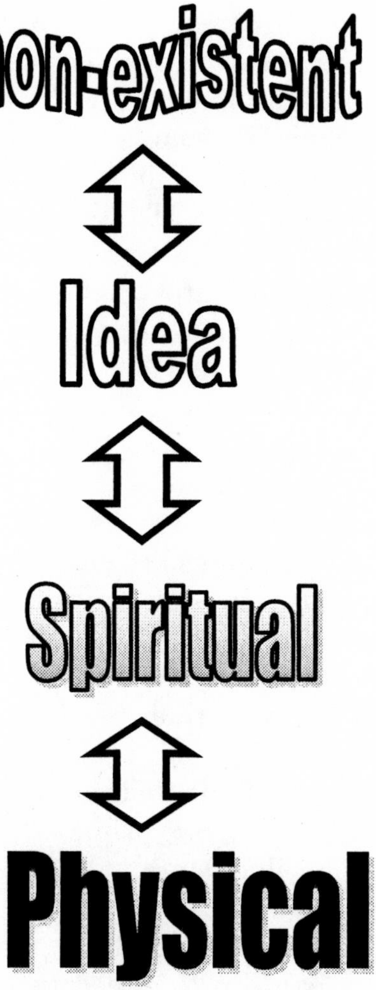

non-existent

⇕

Idea

⇕

Spiritual

⇕

Physical

Our idea takes many forms on its way from being non-existent to being part of our reality in our physical world. Again, the process can reverse at any point along the way.

Fig. 6

From our perspective, figures 5 and 6 are an illustration of the process through which the things we desire come to us. The photograph in front of the pyramids may not be in your scrapbook right now, but at the very least it has moved from being "non-existent" to being an "idea." That's a start!

The Law of Transmutation states that everything, every object, every circumstance, etc., is constantly developing into form or dissipating out of form. When you decide to discard an idea, it ceases to develop and begins to dissipate.

Another way to look at this law is to consider anything living. All living things are either growing or disintegrating. A body starts out invisible, but if you ask any pregnant woman, she'll say there's one coming. Ask any old man if *his* body is coming or going, and he will tell you that his eyesight is going, and that his ability to remember may already be gone. In short, he is disintegrating. We all are, once we have reached our prime. We are on our way back to an "invisible" state.

What about an acorn in your hand? Is it growing or disintegrating? *It is disintegrating,* because it isn't in the right environment for growth. But an acorn in the ground is *growing.* With the right conditions, one day it will be an oak tree.

Ideas are things, too. An idea in its beginning state is invisible in the physical world. The right environment for an idea is our mind. Held there long enough, it begins to move from the invisible to the visible world. Rooted out of our mind by doubt or apathy, the idea is drawn back into an etheric state, to remain invisible forever.

How many times do you have an idea of prosperity, and for a moment you can picture yourself living abundantly, and then the idea goes away because you brush it aside as impractical?

So long as you held the thought in your mind, it was, by law, beginning to be drawn to you. When you let go of the idea, it was drawn away from you. You never saw evidence of it, so you had no idea that what you desired was being affected by your thoughts. These kinds of situations and things are "Perpetually Transmuting." They are constantly coming or going from or toward the physical plane, but we just don't see it happening, so it is naturally easy to doubt. You must believe this law, and you will be able to have the faith you need to hold the idea in your mind until you see fruition.

Although it can be tough to comprehend it, since all we can really see is our physical world, it is important at this point that you accept the more abstract ideas as fact. Just as we cannot "see" the vibrating molecules in a rock, we have learned to accept the fact that there *are* molecules, and that they *do* vibrate. So trust me on this one, and from here we'll be able to build some very powerful ideas to explain the mystery behind prosperity.

> *"Good thoughts and actions can never produce bad results; bad thoughts and actions can never produce good results,* (Allen, 24)...*Men imagine that thought can be kept secret, but it cannot. It rapidly crystallizes into habit, and habit solidifies into circumstance"* (Allen, 28).

Point: In the beginning, all things were first an idea in God's mind. There is an original formless substance or "matter" from which all things are created, and it exists throughout the universe. As Wallace D. Wattles states in his 100 year-old classic, *The Science of Getting Rich:*

> "There is a thinking stuff from which all things are made, and which, in its original state, permeates, penetrates, and fills the interspaces of the universe" (Wattles, Wallace D. 1996. *The Science of Getting Rich.* Phoenix: Life Success Productions, p. 18).

The moment a thought is held in the mind, the formless substance obediently organizes itself to reflect that thought. In due course, the original substance goes from formless to having a spirit form, which reflects the characteristics of the image held in the mind. I believe all things that are physical were first created spiritually this way. Held in the mind long enough with the unwavering belief that it *will* manifest itself in physical form, by law, it is created spiritually and eventually it comes to us physically. By law it must. As we use our thoughts constructively, we are acting as co-creators with God, helping to bring order and form to the formless substance.

Belief is an emotion which speeds the creative process while doubt returns an idea to a formless state. So if you desire something or a circumstance that is good and in harmony with God's desires for you, hold the idea of it in your mind, believing that it is being created and is on its way. The original substance is obedient to the Law of Perpetual Transmutation and the influences of belief and doubt. God understands this law perfectly and uses it to accomplish His purposes as well. It is my personal belief He commands the very elements this way. I believe this is how He organized our world in the beginning. Whether or not it is true, it is an interesting speculation at the very least. However He does it, I'm grateful for the concept because it helps me have faith in His power. It *helps me have faith,* which is precisely what He requires of me before He grants my requests for His blessings.

(Many people of different faiths may say that He established the laws; others say the laws have always existed and He uses them for His purposes. It does not matter which way we believe, these laws can be employed regardless.)

Read the following passages now with this new perspective:

> *"Ask in faith, nothing wavering"* (James 1:6).
>
> *"Delight thyself also in the Lord; and he shall give thee the desires of thine heart. Commit thy way unto the Lord; trust also in him; and he shall bring it to pass"* (Psalms 37:4-5).
>
> *"And all things, whatsoever ye shall ask in prayer, believing, ye shall receive"* (Matthew 21:22).
>
> *"Whatsoever thing ye shall ask in faith, believing that ye shall receive in the name of*

> *Christ, ye shall receive it"* (Enos 1:15, *Book of Mormon*).
>
> *"Whatsoever thing ye shall ask the Father in my name, which is good, in faith believing that ye shall receive, behold, it shall be done unto you"* (Mormon 7:26, *Book of Mormon*).

Let me ask a question: When we pray for something, do we use vain repetitions? (See Matthew 6:7) Perhaps we've done so unknowingly; I know I have. Perhaps you have a desire for which you've asked the Lord time and time again, hoping that your persistence would pay off. When my children do that to me, I call it nagging.

What if we were to take a different approach? What if we try to humbly and sincerely *think* about and visualize what we are asking for? What if we allowed ourselves to really *feel* gratitude for what we need, even before it is with us, as though He has already granted the desires of our heart?

That, my friends, is faith. Imagine one of your children approaching you with gratitude for the sandwich they hope to receive from you. They are already licking their lips as though it was already in their hands, and they only ask once without a question of whether or not you might refuse them.

They have hope and eager anticipation in their eyes. Provided there wasn't a good *reason* to refuse, you'd give them what they ask.

On the other hand, what if a child approached you whining, "*Pleeeeaaaase* I need a sandwich! I'm sooooooo hungry! Why *haven't* you already given me a *sandwich*!? You *knew* I was going to be hungry, where's my sandwich?!"

Do you blame me for thinking there's no *way* I should reward a child for such ingratitude? That child, if he were in my family, would go hungry until he changed his approach. Do I have a sandwich to give? Yes. Do I want the child to have it? Of course! Can I give it to him if he asks improperly? Not if I'm a good parent.

So we should reflect on how we generally approach God in prayer. Do we go to Him, feeling frustrated and upset that He hasn't met our needs yet, and *beg* Him to *please* give us what we ask for, all the while hardly believing He is listening, let alone getting ready to grant our request? Do we find ourselves complaining more than expressing gratitude? Do we feel weary that it has taken him SOOO long to make the changes in our life we want?

What if He was *right there,* ready with that which we desire, prepared to hand it to us the moment or soon after we approach Him with the right attitude: with a grateful and patient heart, genuinely believing we'll receive it because we have already determined through sincere prayer that it is a desire which is in line with His will for us?

What if we asked once, with a heart full of faith, knowing that to ask again could be what He refers to as a vain repetition? After all, He already heard us the first time, and in fact, knew what we needed long before we ever uttered the prayer anyway.

If we asked once, perhaps we could be at peace, knowing it was only a matter of time, because that which we asked for was already on its way. Then we'd begin to move our feet and get to work as though it depended on us.

We'd remind ourselves that He said, "Ask and ye shall receive;" and since we asked, we'd know that we were soon to receive. We wouldn't feel desperate, hoping that our repeated requests were what was needed to get Him to hear us and respond. Ah, let us be careful, lest we nag the Lord...

(Sometimes we can weary Him with our requests, and even if they are not His will for us, He will grant the request and allow us to suffer the natural consequences of failing to trust Him in all things. "Be careful what you pray for;" as they say, "for you just might get it.")

However, to ask once and simply believe isn't all that easy. It's hard to push away the inevitable thoughts of skepticism. But it is possible. With practice, it becomes easier. To be able to recognize doubtful, negative thoughts AND to dismiss them as irrelevant, is a priceless skill indeed...a skill worth developing.

We learn throughout the scriptures how destructive the emotions of doubt and fear can be. On the other hand, we've been taught how powerful faith can be. Now, knowledge of this law of Perpetual Transmutation helps us with our faith. We learn that "believing is seeing," not the other way around.

Brigham Young, the president of the Church of Jesus Christ of Latter-day Saints back in the middle 1800's spoke about what he believed it will be like when we join the Spirit World. In doing so, he revealed a powerful truth that puts these ideas into perspective. He said:

> "If we want to visit Jerusalem, or this, that, or the other place—and I presume we will be permitted if we desire—there we are, looking at its streets. If we want to behold Jerusalem as it was in the days of the Savior; or if we want to see the Garden of Eden as it was when created, there we are, and we see it as it existed spiritually, *for it was created first spiritually and then temporally, and spiritually it still remains*" (*Teachings of the Presidents of the Church, BRIGHAM YOUNG*, Salt Lake City, Utah: The Church of Jesus Christ of Latter-day Saints, p. 281).

An idea held in the right environment (your mind) will begin to take form. It is only in the *last stage* of the process that you will "see" it. Do not reverse the process with doubt or fear. Belief and faith bring it into form; doubt and fear return it to the invisible.

In fact, I've noticed that many times I will have a thought which I may entertain for a while, and imagine how it would feel if it should it come true...but then life goes on and I forget the situation I had imagined. Without consciously discarding the idea at some point along the way as impossible, many times I have found the situation came true, all on its own, even though I hadn't spent a whole lot of time trying to make it happen. I suppose that seed was of a variety that didn't require a whole lot of attention, like a palm tree in the desert. The seed had been planted, and NOT uprooted, therefore it grew. All on its own, it grew. All I had to do was imagine it, feel the emotion I expected to feel, and then let it grow by leaving it alone, doubting not.

Isn't this amazing? If you think the first law was intriguing, *just wait, it gets better!*

LESSON 2:

LAW OF RELATIVITY

Occasionally we find ourselves in disagreeable circumstances. It is natural to think, "My life stinks; everything's going wrong." Well, don't forget Lesson 1, the Law of Perpetual Transmutation. These are thoughts, too, and if we allow ourselves to hold *these* kinds of thoughts in our mind, and allow ourselves to believe them, then, by law, the formless substance starts to be obedient and eventually your circumstances will be a reflection of *these* thoughts.

The Law of Relativity is useful for helping to keep good thoughts in your mind. **The Law states that nothing we experience is fundamentally good or bad**. Bad things that happen to us are only bad relative to something better. If you are convinced that you are dealing with a rotten circumstance, then you need to ask God to help you *see* it differently. Compare your situation to something much worse, and you will be able to maintain more faithful thoughts. That is the goal.

Some of the earliest pioneer settlers of the American West traveled with handcarts instead of horse-drawn carriages. They were religious refugees, seeking a place where they would not be persecuted for their beliefs. Their leaders had organized numerous groups to travel together. While many came in covered wagons, others were short on time as well as supplies, and began their journey with handcarts. One particular company was called the Martin Handcart Company, which was organized to leave late in the summer from Iowa. The members of the company were caught in early snows near the Continental Divide in 1856 before being rescued, and their suffering was unlike any of us today can comprehend.

I want to take you on a piece of their journey. Put yourself in their shoes. Pay close attention to your feelings as you visualize what you are reading. It is important for this lesson that you concentrate as you read, rather than just skimming the words and glossing over them.

When they say "Mother," think of your *own* mother. When they say "I," let it be *you*, etc. At the end of this discussion, we will be going through an exercise to help drive this law home. Since this book is intended to make a difference and since a difference in your life relies on a switch in your thinking, there will never be a better time than right here, right now to *try* it. Practice exercising your mental faculties by visualizing and allowing yourself to *experience* what you are reading. This one thing may be the most important thing you do during this time you're already investing to read this book.

Let's begin the journey…

John Kirkman: "Before we left Iowa, my dear Mother had given birth to a son, Peter. She was naturally weak with the care of a nursing baby and five other children. Father was weak from want of food, having denied himself for us. The terrible strain of the journey was too much for him and one night, near the Sweetwater, he passed quietly away at the age of 35. Our little brother, Peter, died the same night. They built a fire to thaw the ground so that a grave could be dug, then with my baby brother clasped in his arms, they wrapped him in a blanket and laid him tenderly away. My darling Mother had to take up the journey alone with us five children. Provisions were almost gone, desolation reigned.

"The company passed off the main road to 'Martin's Ravine' to escape the terrible blizzards and storms for we had little clothing and had given up all hope. Death had taken a heavy toll and the Ravine was like an overcrowded tomb. No mortal tongue could describe the suffering" (Cook, Mary Larson Kirkman Hulet. 1998. *Woman of Faith and Fortitude, Daughters of Utah Pioneers,* used with permission).

Elizabeth Sermon: "My husband's health began to fail and his heart almost broken to see me falling in shafts. Myself and children hungry, almost naked, footsore and himself nearly done for. Many trials came after this. My oldest boy had the mountain fever, we had to haul him in the cart, there was not room in the wagon. One day we started him out before the carts in the morning to walk with the aged and sick, but we had not gone far on our journey before we found him lying by the roadside, unable to go any farther. I picked him up and put him on my back and drew my cart as well, but could not manage far, so put him in the cart, which made three children and my luggage. My husband failing more each day, the Captain put a young man to help me for a short time. My other son Henry walked at 7 years old, 1,300 miles with the exception of a few miles…

"I will here state there was no time in crossing the rivers to stop and take off clothing, but we had to wade through and draw our carts at the same time with our clothes dripping wet...

"My husband's sufferings have always pained me and I can never forget them. Poor Rob's [age 5] feet began to freeze. I cannot remember the place; it was after wading a very deep river [Platte?] the freezing commenced. We had no wood but sagebrush. I went out and cut the sage to keep the fire all night. Covered them up with their feet to the fire and cut some more and kept the fire as well as I could. My clothes froze stiff. Well, we got through that night. Your father would not walk now. He would get into wagon after wagon, only to be turned out. The cattle were giving out and everyone had their friends, but the friend death, would soon end his sufferings. John [age 9] and Rob had to ride, Henry [age 7] walked, your father would take my arm and walk a little distance, fall on his knees with weakness. We moved from Devil's Gate.

"After our food had given out as I said before, we went into our tents to die. I always thought I could get through to Salt Lake City and I tried to encourage my husband, but he was starving. He had always lived good at home....

"Your father after having some food and clothes, seemed to revive. He called you to him and told you to be good children and to do all you could for me, and then he said to me, 'God bless you, Eli,' that being the name he called me. 'You have saved my life this time.' I said, 'We must hold out now and get to the wagons,' but we had to go back to the 1/4 lb. of flour and he sank under it. I think he would not have died if he had got food, but he was spared the trial ahead. We went to bed about 3:00. He put his arm around me and said, 'I am done,' and breathed his last.

“Father was buried in the morning with 2 more in the grave. I stood like a statue, bewildered, not a tear: the cold chills, even now as I write, creep over my body, for I feel I can still see the wolves waiting for their bodies as they would come down to camp before we left.

“When I got into camp I found it some help to toast the rawhide on the coals and chew it; it helped to keep the hunger away, for I was feeling it rather keenly now. I had to take a portion of poor Robert's feet off which pierced my very soul. I had to sever the leaders with a pair of scissors. Little did I think when I bought them in old England that they would be used for such a purpose. Every day some portion was decaying until the poor boy's feet were all gone. Then John's began to freeze; then afterwards my own....

“Poor Brother Blair, a very tall thin man; he was starving and was eating a piece of griddle cake; another poor brother, not as hungry asked for a piece of it. He said, 'I cannot do it, I want it myself.' Poor fellow he died in the night and so one after another passed away. Fathers, mothers, sisters, brothers and friends, many, many honest souls laid in mother earth....

“A severe storm came up. I think it was on the Sweetwater, but I was so troubled I forget all about the names of places. My eldest boy John's feet decaying, my boys both of them losing their limbs, their father dead, my own feet very painful, I thought, 'Why can't I die?'” (Glazer, Stewart E. and Robert S. Clark, eds., *Journal of the Trail* 2nd ed. [1997], 103–107; paragraphing altered. Held in the Joel Ricks collection at Utah State University, used with permission.)

Are you taking time to feel a portion of what they felt? One more to go....

Ephraim Hanks: "I reached the ill-fated train just as the immigrants were camping for the night. The sight that met my gaze as I entered their camp can never be erased from my memory. The starved forms and haggard countenances of the poor sufferers, as they moved about slowly, shivering with cold, to prepare their scanty evening meal, was enough to touch the stoutest heart. When they saw me coming, they hailed me with joy inexpressible, and when they further beheld the supply of fresh meat I brought into camp, their gratitude knew no bounds. Flocking around me, one would say, 'Oh, please, give me a small peace of meat;' another would exclaim, 'My poor children are starving, do give me a little;' and children with tears in their eyes would call out, 'Give me some, give me some.' At first I tried to wait on them and handed out the meat as they called for it; but finally I told them to help themselves. Five minutes later both my horses had been released of their extra burden—the meat was all gone.

"I have but a very little to say about the sufferings of Captain Martin's company before I joined it; but it had passed through terrible ordeals. Women and the larger children helped the men to pull the hand-carts, and in crossing the frozen streams, they had to break the ice with their feet. In fording the Platte River, the largest stream they had to cross after the cold weather set in, the clothes of the immigrants were frozen stiff around their bodies before they could exchange them for others. This is supposed to have been the cause of the many deaths, which occurred soon afterwards. It has been stated on good authority that nineteen immigrants died one night.

"The survivors who performed the last acts of kindness to those who perished, were not strong enough to dig the graves of sufficient depth to preserve the bodies from the wild beasts, and wolves were actually seen tearing open the graves before the company was out of sight.

"Many of the survivors, in witnessing the terrible afflictions and losses, became at last almost stupefied or mentally dazed." (Andrew Jenson, *The Contributor,* February, 1893, vol. XIL, pp. 202-5, as quoted by Stewart E. Glazier, ed., *Journal of the Trail* [Salt Lake City, Utah: 1996], 94-98.)

What is your biggest challenge right now? What would these immigrants have to say about the load you are carrying? What are your feelings about what *they* had to endure? Read on...

At a later time, there was a meeting where some people were expressing criticism that church leadership had allowed the Martin handcart company to leave so late into the season. A man who had been in that company and was listening to their comments was finally compelled to stand and speak his mind. He asked the people to please stop, and in so many words he told them that they had no knowledge of what they were talking about. He said the facts and details of the experience were meaningless because they didn't provide proper context of the issues at hand. Was it a mistake to go so late? Yes, his sufferings were unspeakable and many did not survive...but he asked if they ever heard any of the survivors speak a word of criticism. No, they had not; and neither did any of the company leave the Church. Imagine that. He said that because of their experiences they developed an absolute assurance that God lives, *for they developed a strong, personal, enduring relationship with Him through their adversities.* (Derived from the account as told by James E. Faust in The Refiner's Fire. *Ensign,* May 1979.)

I'm reminded of Job's similar response to Zophar the Naamathite. Job said:

> "Hold your peace, let me alone, that I may speak, and let come on me what *will.* Wherefore do I take my flesh in my teeth, and put my life in mine hand? Though he slay me, yet will I trust in him" (Job 13:13-15).

I don't know how easy it was for the man in the handcart company to feel gratitude while he was still on the trek. But in hindsight he was able to recognize the blessing which came out of the adversity.

What if we could have foresight about what our hindsight will be?

If we can know we'll always be able to look back with gratitude, then maybe we can let ourselves feel that gratitude a little early. Gratitude always pleases God, and He will always bless us for our expressions of gratitude.

In hindsight, the man said that at times he was so weary that he'd look ahead at a hill or patch of sand, determined to go just that far, and then give up because he knew he wouldn't be able to pull the load through it. However, when he reached the slope or sand pit, *there* is where it seemed the *cart began to push him*. As retold by David O. McKay, the man said, "I have looked back many times to see who was pushing my cart, but my eyes saw no one" (Faust, James E. 1979. The Refiner's Fire. *Ensign,* May). As you can see, the general feeling held by this gentleman was definitely not one of bitterness. He concluded that the price he paid was a "privilege to pay," because through it he became acquainted with God Himself.

What an amazing attitude toward adversity. The more submissive we are to God, I believe the more grateful we can be in our challenges. We can trust that under any circumstance, He has our best interest at heart. We will not always understand His ways, but to trust Him as we are led along through life's lessons brings immeasurable peace. We can have *gratitude* for our present conditions, no matter what they are, because it is the lessons of the present that prepare us for the blessings of the future.

More about Job: We cannot discuss this lesson without mentioning more about the story of Job from the Bible. Job truly has to be the most unfortunate man that ever lived, until his adversity was well behind him. He had everything anyone could ever want, and bit by bit the Lord allowed it all to be taken away. His wealth, his family, his friends, his health...nevertheless, take a look at how he handled it. In his words:

> "...the Lord gave, and the Lord hath taken away; blessed be the name of the Lord" (Job 1:21).

> "What? shall we receive good at the hand of God, and shall we not receive evil?" (Job 2:10)

Even when he was overcome with grief from his suffering, he cursed the day he was born, but never cursed God.

> "After this opened Job his mouth, and cursed his day. And Job spake, and said, Let the day perish wherein I was born" (Job 3:1-3).

In the end, the Lord prospered Job from 7,000 to 14,000 sheep; 3,000 to 6,000 camels; 500 to 1,000 yoke of oxen; and 500 to 1,000 she asses. (See Job chapters 1 and 42) Similarly, we can prosper, as we choose to look for the good in any given situation. God appreciates our gratitude and rewards us for it sooner or later. It's not just a great bedtime story...it's in the Bible to teach us how we might live a more blessed life. We are rewarded immediately with peace and in time with prosperity as well, if we seek wealth the Lord's way.

So, what about the Law? This is the Law of Relativity. You want better circumstances. Everybody does, but we must first begin by seeking peace in our present circumstances. We must feel gratitude for all of the blessings that we already enjoy. I've heard it said, "I complained that I had no shoes until I met a man who had no feet." The Law of Relativity is a tool to help us find gratitude.

It gives us a way to think more cheerfully, and thus be prepared for greater blessings.

> "Be filled with the Spirit...Giving thanks always for all things unto God and the Father in the name of the Lord Jesus Christ" (Ephesians 5:18, 20).

Do not use the Law of Relativity against yourself. You could do this very easily by comparing your situation to better ones. We are to think of better circumstances as the first step to having them, but we do not think of them to make ourselves feel bad about where we are. We think of them with hope and gratitude that we will eventually enjoy them in reality. Use the Law of Relativity to aid you in keeping positive thoughts. As you do, the Law of Perpetual Transmutation from Chapter 1 will ensure that better circumstances are truly on their way.

Is there ever an opportunity to commiserate without sabotaging our overall objective? Perhaps...It seems I've heard of one very practical way that Dr. Stephen R. Covey (best-selling author of *7 Habits of Highly Effective Families*) handled complaining in his family. As the story goes, when they hiked together, they didn't tolerate whining from their children. But at one point he let them all have a break to rest, whereupon they were encouraged to complain as much as they needed to. “Oh my feet are *killing* me!” “How much *farth*er?” “I’m so *tired.*” Whatever they wanted to say all along, here was their opportunity. And with everyone letting it go at the same time, they eventually became bored, and realized how pathetic they all sounded. Finally, as a result, they were able to move on cheerfully. The way that they saw their burdens changed. The burden didn’t change, but they way they handled it did.

These ideas are not the typical automatic response, just as an ambulance won’t automatically come without someone first placing a 911 call. We have to choose to fight the natural tendencies we all have, or give them controlled release, as Dr. Covey demonstrates. But it gets easier with practice, so we must never give up trying. Some circumstances will not change in this life, but how we *feel* about them can. How we deal with them can change for the better. Sometimes it is after we allow ourselves to feel differently that we finally receive the blessing we seek.

According to the Book of Mormon, there was a group of people who lived about 120 B.C. on the American Continent who experienced this process of change as I have just described. Here is an excerpt from the Book of Mosiah within the Book of Mormon. This segment of the story has inspired me and given me faith when I am have been in the middle of overwhelming challenges:

> "And it came to pass that so great were their afflictions that they began to cry mightily to God. And Amulon commanded them that they should stop their cries; and he put guards over them to watch them, that whosoever should be found calling upon God should be put to death. And Alma and his people did not raise their voices to the Lord their God, but did pour out their hearts to him; and he did know the thoughts of their hearts. And it came to pass that the voice of the Lord came to them in their afflictions, saying: Lift up your heads and be of good comfort, for I know of the covenant which ye have made unto me; and I will covenant with my people and deliver them out of bondage.
>
> "And I will also ease the burdens which are put upon your shoulders, that even you cannot feel them upon your backs, even while you are in bondage; and this will I do that ye may stand as witnesses for me hereafter, and that ye may know of a surety

that I, the Lord God, do visit my people in their afflictions.

"And now it came to pass that the burdens which were laid upon Alma and his brethren were made light; yea, the Lord did strengthen them that they could bear up their burdens with ease, and they did submit cheerfully and with patience to all the will of the Lord…

"And in the morning the Lord caused a deep sleep to come upon the Lamanites, yea, and all their task-masters were in a profound sleep. And Alma and his people departed into the wilderness; and when they had traveled all day they pitched their tents in a valley, and they called the valley Alma, because he led their way in the wilderness.

"Yea, and in the valley of Alma they poured out their thanks to God because he had been merciful unto them, and eased their burdens, and had delivered them out of bondage; for they were in bondage, and none could deliver them except it were the Lord their God. And they gave thanks to God, yea, all their men and all their women and all their children that could speak lifted their voices in the

> praises of their God" (Mosiah 24:10-15, 19-22, paragraphing altered).

What if the Lord could help *us* feel our burdens differently? Through knowledge of the Law of Relativity, He's helped me do that now and then, and I believe it can help you, too. Try. Just try it for a few minutes. Feel some gratitude, *for something*. If you skip this exercise, you run the risk of having nothing change about the extent to which the Lord is able to bless you.

Lesson 3 will teach you how you can use this principle to begin attracting more favorable circumstances to you, and best of all…what is going on "behind the scenes," so to speak, to make it happen.

LESSON 3:
LAW OF VIBRATION

This law states that not only is **everything in a state of vibration**, but that **vibration is a medium for transferring signals**. Let's break it down.

Flashback to 9th Grade Chemistry: We already know from science that everything is vibrating. Solids, liquids, and gasses are all made up of molecules that are in a continual state of movement. The faster the vibration, the more fluid a substance is. Water is made up of two hydrogen molecules joined with one oxygen molecule. If these molecules are vibrating at a very slow rate, then the water is in the form of ice. When the air molecules around the ice are moving very rapidly, then, as they bump up against the surface of the ice, that movement is transferred to the water molecules, and they also begin to move more rapidly. This is what is actually happening when warm air begins to melt a piece of ice. There is a transfer of energy from one substance to another, through vibration. Eventually the ice becomes water this way, and if energy in the form of heat continues to increase the rate of vibration of the water, then the molecules will vibrate so rapidly that they will begin to break apart and become steam, and then vapor. The water still exists, but the molecules are so far apart now that we do not see them as water as we know it any longer. This is a little reminiscent of Lesson 1, isn't it?

Part two of the law is that vibration is a medium for transferring signals. In a way, we have discussed how heat can be transferred from one substance to another through vibration. Now, we are going to look at how *signals* are transferred through vibration.

One example of vibrations around us is in telecommunications. I'm not going to get real scientific about this part, but I think you'll agree that there are signals all around us that we cannot see, which are transferred through the medium of vibration. There are microwaves, radio waves, whatever cell phones do.... My husband connects to the Internet while we're driving down Main Street. Wireless! Even fiber optics use impulses to transfer data, which is another form of repetitive movement, or vibration. Color, light, sound...these are all demonstrations of vibration.

When we see two different colors or hear different kinds of sounds, we know it is the variations in wavelengths which distinguish the difference.

Did you know? Red has a wavelength of approximately 700 nanometers, while violet has a wavelength of approximately 400 nanometers. The other visible colors have wavelengths which lie somewhere between these figures.

When I turn on a radio, and tune in to a station, I hear music. Did I pull the music into the room by turning on the radio? No, the music was already there, the machine just made it audible. It went from inaudible to audible by adjusting the tool. Because of these invisible signals, I can take a little gadget, punch in a handful of numbers and speak to a specifically chosen individual on the other side of the planet. The mind of man created the tool, is there any question that the mind of man has the capacity to **be** such a tool? It's a stretch to comprehend it, but worth considering nonetheless.

This brings to mind of one of my favorite poems. The poet, Carol Lynn Pearson, has given me permission to include it here. It is titled "Prayer:"

This radio set called prayer
Is designed for remarkably simple repair.
When the lines fail, there is no doubt
Which half of the set is out.
(Carol Lynn Pearson, *Prayer)*

Our spirits have a body equipped with a brain. We are God's crowning creation. We can learn how to use the inherent powers He gave us. As you read on, you'll discover that this is all really very simple. It does not require great efforts in telepathy or anything strange. You are using yourself as this "tool" all the time already. But understanding how it operates helps you take better control of the circumstances in your life. It lends to peace and eliminates fear to understand these principles. Read on....

So here we sit, inside this body we were given at birth. As infants, it was all we could do to learn how to get those little fingers into that mouth. We'd spend all day long trying to fire the right neurons to control the right muscles in perfect balance to achieve the desired results. In this way we learned how to crawl, and walk, and create vibrations with our vocal chords in ways that helped us get what we wanted. As we grew, we got better at all of it. At some point in time, most of us quit exercising our mind to see what else it could help us do. We were satisfied with the circumstances we were in. We had food when we needed it, we got where we needed to go, and we knew how to get everything that a baby could ever want, all on our own.

What about now? Are you satisfied? Do you live the kind of life you'd like to live? What would you change? Just because we "grew up," it doesn't mean there isn't more for us to learn about the tools God gave us at birth. He has said over and over that we need to be as little children. Little children are eager to learn, and are never satisfied. Don't misunderstand, we can be happy and grateful for all He has given us, but to be satisfied is the beginning of decline. In speaking to the Philippians, Paul said:

> "I know both how to be abased, and I know how to abound: every where and in all things I am *instructed both to be full and to be hungry, both to abound and to suffer need*" (Philippians 4:12, italics added).

As children of God, we have within us creative powers. That was a characteristic that we inherited from the Father. When a child takes a crayon and designs a picture unlike any other that has ever been put to paper, that child is demonstrating that she has a portion of God's creative powers within her. Maybe it is a purple giraffe. Isn't that exciting? I never quite celebrated creativity the way I do now. It begins in the mind. She saw something in her mind, and held it there until she saw it on her paper. Her hand knew just what to do, and it got better with practice, didn't it?

Now take a moment and visualize the way you'd like your life to be. Be like that little girl with the purple giraffe in her mind. It doesn't have to seem real, or even possible; it only has to be vivid. Exercise the creative faculties in your mind to come up with a wonderful new picture for your life. Take a moment to write down, with detail, the idea that you just created.

A New Picture for my Life (written in present-tense, as though it were already true)

(a new picture for my life, continued…)

Stay with me on this, I think you'll find a powerful paradigm shift as I bring it all together....

Now, read this carefully: **The physical counterpart of your collection of non-physical ideas *has a specific vibration* that distinguishes it from anything else**. Just as a red light has a specific wavelength, and just as a cell phone in Tibet has a specific identifier, so also does everything and every situation in the world have a specific "vibration." Feeling skeptical? Keep reading... (and wipe that quirky look off your face; it's revealing your vibration ☺).

> "The outer conditions of a person's life will always be found to be harmoniously related to his inner state...The soul attracts that which it secretly harbors; that which it loves, and also that which it fears...Men do not attract that which they want, but that which they are" (Allen, 18).

Do you realize what this means? This means that life as you know it is already in perfect harmony with the thoughts and feelings stored in your mind from years, months, days, or even just moments ago. Whether or not you like your circumstances, on a subconscious level, you *are right at home*.

So what's the goal? To put *ourselves*, our bodies, this gift we were given at birth, into a vibration that is in *harmony* with the thing or circumstance we *desire*, instead of the circumstances we already have.

When I first learned that I was in complete harmony with my financially stressful life, I fought the idea. There was no way I could be "comfortable" with things as they were, on a subconscious level! I was so completely frustrated with my circumstances; how on earth could I be "at home" with them and not even realize it?!

Then I began to pay attention to my thoughts and feelings, and began to force myself to daydream and *feel* what it might be like to enjoy life the way I really wanted it. Such a simple task, but so hard to do if you aren't used to doing it. I discovered that pretty soon, new ideas began to come my way… new opportunities, new people, and new hope.

If you, on the other hand, are convinced that your surroundings are definitely *out of harmony* with who you are, then ask yourself, "When was the last time I visualized life as I really *want* it, and allowed myself to *feel* the way I expect it to feel if it were already true?

If you've done that, and allowed yourself to believe that the new circumstances are truly on their way, and if you feel more emotion related to life as you *want* it than you do about life as it *is*, then it is only a matter of time before your circumstances will finally reflect the thoughts of your heart. **By allowing yourself to *feel* the new circumstances, you are putting yourself in vibration which is harmonious with the circumstance you seek.** It will be drawn to you as naturally as moths to a light bulb.

Emotion is the key. Whatever your dominant emotion is, is what determines your future. In other words, if you feel grateful and excited about a prosperous future, but *more often* feel a stronger emotion of anxiety and worry about *financial bondage* in your future, the negative emotions will keep you in harmonious vibration with a state of financial bondage and stress.

Practice gratitude. Practice daydreaming about life the way you *want* it… soon you'll have changed the condition of your heart, and as we know, "as a man thinketh in his heart, so is he…" (Proverbs 23:7). It's only a matter of time.

Putting yourself in harmony with a certain type of situation in an effort to bring it to you, is not unlike how the attraction of two different physical objects work. When two objects or substances are in harmonious vibration, (meaning, their frequency is compatible) then they are drawn together. Water will adhere to just about anything it touches, but if you take a droplet of water, and a droplet of vegetable oil and bring them together, there is absolutely no attraction. They are not in harmonious vibration.

I can't tell you how to measure the difference in vibration between, say, a run-down, greasy fast food restaurant and an exclusive gourmet "*ristorante.*" But I can feel it. I think you can too. I can't say how to measure the difference between the vibration of a 1969 Volkswagen Beetle and this year's model of the top of the line Mercedes, but I know there is one. Different genres of music all have a different "feel" as well.

According to one of my many mentors, Bob Proctor, **A "feeling" is nothing more than a conscious awareness of a particular vibration**. Digest *that* idea for a minute...

Do you doubt that you are in a certain vibration? You can sense other people's vibrations. You can sense when someone is looking at you from behind. Someone comes in the room with a negative vibe, and you may ask, "What's wrong?" and they might say, "Nothing." But, you know they are lying because even the *dog* knows something is wrong!

The kind of "vibration" that we're in is changeable, and within our control. We change our vibration by changing our thoughts and the feelings generated by those thoughts.

Too often our prayers and our thoughts (not to mention our actions) are sometimes out of harmony with each other. For our prayers to be effective, all three aspects must be in agreement with each other.

> "Not what he wishes and prays for does a man get, but what he justly earns. His wishes and prayers are only gratified and answered when they harmonize with his thoughts and actions" (Allen, 18).

A religious application of this 'vibration' concept: The nature of our thoughts will also be a huge factor in whether or not we are able to become "in tune" with the Spirit of God. We must discipline and purify our thoughts, and feel gratitude (I mean *really feel* gratitude for something) and then it becomes easier to feel and recognize communication from Him. He promises us: "Draw near unto me and I will draw near unto you," (Doctrine & Covenants 88:63).

When I conduct seminars, I like to illustrate this with two large tuning forks. If they are in tune, then I can strike one with a mallet, and the other one will actually begin to sing. If they are not in tune, then you can strike one with the mallet and the other will stay silent. It is all about the Law of Vibration.

As one of my favorite speakers, John Bytheway, points out, this is how two people sitting in a church meeting can feel completely different about what is being said. If you are in tune with the Spirit, it does not matter who is speaking or *what* is being said, the Spirit *will* communicate with you, directly.

A perfect example of this: one person saw a church *leader* visit a children's meeting and *take notes* fervently as the young child gave a simple talk about God's plan from the tiny pulpit. The leader was *in tune* with the Spirit, so her simple words carried powerful meaning to his heart through the Spirit of God.

Back to our discussion of being "in harmony" with a desired *circumstance*: In terms of being "in tune" with the circumstances you desire, it is important to realize that whatever thing or circumstance you desire has a certain vibratory characteristic. Furthermore, when you are finally in harmony with it, it will come to you. If you are *not* in harmony with it, though it be right there available to you, it will pass on by. In fact, once you are in harmony with it, you'll *feel* it coming, even before it is with you. You'll just know it's on its way.

Additionally, it's important to realize that *there is abundance*. Nobody lacks because the supply is lacking. There is more than enough of everything we could want. There is plenty to go around, and if it should run out, more would be created from the same raw material God used to create the world. So don't think you lack because "there is lack." There isn't. There is only abundance. Sterling W. Sill, a now deceased member of the Council of the Twelve Apostles of the Church of Jesus Christ of Latter-day Saints wrote:

> "Think of the lavish abundance with which creation surrounds us. Everything we could possibly wish for has been placed within our easy reach. It was certainly intended that

> everyone who wished it should have an abundance" (Sill, Sterling W. 1975. *The Laws of Success,* Salt Lake City: Deseret Book, p. 13).

So why do we experience lack? We only lack because we are not yet in harmony with the abundance we desire.

Whoa! Heavy stuff, I know! Let's take a break for a story to illustrate.

Christmas Wish which Came True: One year my children really wanted some Lego™ sets ("Lego" is a trademark for The Lego Group toy company, Denmark). My oldest had at least three particular sets in mind, each costing up to fifty dollars. Economically, I had a hard time justifying such a purchase. But I taught him to write down what he desired, and believe.

No, I wasn't going to just supply it; I wanted him to learn the power behind applying these principles. Several times he came to me distraught because he knew I wasn't going to buy them, and doubted the principles. Each time I just encouraged him to believe, and to imagine how awesome it would feel to get the blessing he desired. Sometimes I also felt doubt, but proactively pushed that emotion aside, knowing that there really is no harm in just believing. **When I have a choice, I choose to believe.**

For all I knew, he'd get creative and think of a way to earn a bunch of money and buy them himself...which was a stretch to consider, since even I couldn't think of a single thing to do to create an extra hundred and fifty dollars.

We had a very *small* set of Legos which were twenty-five years old. Very basic: just blocks and wheels. My son wanted the building blocks with all the bells and whistles. He had his sights fixed on the specialized kinds; the pirates, the animals, the works. He decided in his own nine year-old way that he was no longer in "harmonious vibration" with the plain old Lego set.

I brought my children together and said, "If you want the better blocks, then you need to make a place for them. Grandma would like this old set for when her grandkids come to visit, would you be willing to give her your old set? That way we have a place for new ones." (There is a brief explanation of the "Sea of Galilee" principle behind that idea at the end of this chapter, and the Vacuum Law of Prosperity at the end of the book.)

In the meantime, my husband and I shopped the online auctions, looking for a phenomenal deal on a huge pile of Lego blocks.

Then one day at work, a co-worker approached my husband and said, "My twelve-year-old son has a bunch of Lego blocks that he doesn't use anymore, could your kids use them?" This came from out of the blue, like vapor gathers into a cloud. In fact, by the time he arranged to take them, she had contacted her relatives and they had contributed all of theirs as well. Four massive boxes full: pirates, animals, spacemen, spaceships, castles...more than $1,000.00 worth. The idea cloud became heavy and oh, how it rained Legos that day! Our Father in Heaven is good, isn't He?! You should have seen my children's faces on Christmas morning. We were just as excited for them, as they were for themselves.

I mentioned this experience to my friend, and she said, "We did the same thing for a snowboard!" And I thought, *how interesting*. We had no inclination toward getting a snowboard, but they did. They had no inclination toward Legos, but we did. We both got what we wanted. We both received that which was in harmony with the thoughts and intents of our hearts.

> *"If a son shall ask bread of any of you that is a father, will he give him a stone? or if he ask a fish, will he for a fish give him a serpent?"* (Luke 11:11)

> *"And all things, whatsoever ye shall ask in prayer, believing, ye shall receive"* (Matthew 21:22).

Then there's the story of our suburban. I won't get into it here, but I have to say, that until I fixed the idea in my mind and held it there long enough, I would not have been comfortable in the newer suburban. It was "too nice for the likes of me," until I allowed myself to think differently. It is all about vibration. Holding the image of what you want in your mind, and then *feeling* the gratitude you expect to feel when it is yours, you move your "tool," your body, into a vibration that is in harmony with what you desire.

I remember the day when my husband announced as we barreled down the freeway in the old, beat up, brown suburban, "I am NO longer in harmonious vibration with this suburban!" I, on the other hand, was fine with it. I despised how it looked, but didn't want to be ungrateful. It took me some time before I felt okay about looking for a way to own something a little more dependable, and a lot more beautiful.

How is it drawn to you? Like a radio transmitter, we send out vibrations. Those vibrations just fly on by as they pass things that are not in tune with your frequency. But they resonate with things that *are* in tune. People, situations, things…anything we need to have our desire fulfilled will be drawn to us when we are "in tune" with that which we desire.

Now go back in your mind to the first part of this law, which states: everything vibrates. Remember things that vibrate rapidly are more fluid (or even outright invisible), than the same thing vibrating more slowly. Your thoughts are flighty, are they not? Or, am I the only one that struggles to focus on any one thought? Well, here's something to think about: thoughts are things that are at a very high rate of vibration. Essentially, they are invisible. We would like to see them become "real." (That's kind of a funny way to put it…it is like saying ice is real but vapor isn't, which is ridiculous, actually. Your thoughts are just as real as vapor is.)

As you hold them in your mind and allow yourself to *feel how it will be* when they are with you, you are putting yourself in a vibration that is in harmony with the physical counterpart of that idea. If it already exists in physical form somewhere, then the vibrations you send out are putting into motion the events necessary to bring it to you. If it does not already exist, then your thought is directly responsible for the co-creation of the thing.

You will be drawn to the people or things you need to cause its creation. This is a Law you can depend on. Really! You can count on it! There is no need for fear, or worry, or doubt. These are negative vibrations that repel the very things you want and need. Why sabotage the creative process?

A word about what we deserve.... Should we want better things? Do we deserve a better life? We are children of a God! He would have us enjoy all the blessings we are capable of appreciating. But we need to allow ourselves to feel comfortable with more. To think that the nicer suburban was "too good for me" was a borderline insult to God; as if His child wasn't worth having a respectable vehicle. I know if any of *my* children were to turn away a gift with the comment, "I'm not good enough for something so nice," I would feel sadness. Wouldn't you?

You may wish for a nicer home, but if you keep thinking you don't deserve one, you'll never receive it. Even if you did, you wouldn't feel at home there, it just wouldn't *feel* right.

God cannot bless you with something if you are repelling it. It would violate law for Him to do so.

"Doubt not!" "Fear not!" Oh, how He wants to bless you! All you have to do is believe, and He will do it! "Doubt not!" "Fear not!" *It's not good for you! You'll wish you hadn't!*

> *"For verily I say unto you, That whosoever shall say unto this mountain, Be thou removed, and be thou cast into the sea; and shall not doubt in his heart, but shall believe that those things which he saith shall come to pass; he shall have whatsoever he saith"* (Mark 11:23).

> *"Fear thou not, for I am with thee; be not dismayed for I am thy God: I will strengthen thee; yea, I will help thee"* (Isaiah 41:10).

> *"Fear not, little flock; for it is your Father's good pleasure to give you the kingdom"* (Luke 12:32).

Is my idea okay? Do you worry that you shouldn't desire something that is not God's will for you?

That is a worthy concern, for "*What shall it profit a man, if he shall gain the whole world, and lose his own soul?*" (Mark 8:36)

You're always invited to determine if something is in harmony with God's will for you. This can only increase your faith that you will receive it, so *by all means, pray about it.*

How can you recognize an answer? Determine in your own mind what you think is right, and then go to Him and tell him what you have concluded. Then ask if your conclusion is accurate, and pay attention to your feelings. If it is right, you will feel peace and love. If it is wrong, you will feel nothing or confusion. Trust these feelings; accept them as literal communication with your Father in Heaven.

Oh what comfort there is in genuine, humble prayer.

> *"Behold, you have not understood; you have supposed that I would give it unto you, when you took no thought save it was to ask me. But, behold, I say unto you, that you must study it out in your mind; then you must ask me if it be right, and if it is right I will cause that your bosom shall burn within you; therefore, you shall feel that it is right. But if*

> *it be not right you shall have no such feelings, but you shall have a stupor of thought that shall cause you to forget the thing which is wrong"* (Doctrine and Covenants 9:7-9).

In fact, as you make attempts to find answers through prayer, remember this: we have a radio set called prayer. Successful communication with God does not depend on Him; it depends on us. He stands at the door and knocks, but He does not force Himself in. We must put *ourselves* in tune with *Him*. How? **We change our vibration through deep and profound gratitude**

Remember the Law of Relativity, which helps us accomplish this. Always express sincere gratitude in prayer before presenting requests. It helps us be in tune and better prepared for an answer.

Moroni in the Book of Mormon once said this about the doctrines of the gospel:

> "Behold, I would exhort you that when ye shall read these things, if it be wisdom in God that ye should read them, that ye would remember how merciful the Lord hath been unto the children of men, from the creation of Adam even down until the time that ye

> shall receive these things, and ponder it in your hearts."

He says we must do that *before* asking God if something is true or not. He continues:

> "And when ye shall receive these things, I would exhort you that ye would ask God, the Eternal Father, in the name of Christ, if theses things are not true; and if ye shall ask with a sincere heart, with real intent, having faith in Christ, he will manifest the truth of it unto you, by the power of the Holy Ghost. And by the power of the Holy Ghost *ye may know the truth of all things*" (Moroni 10:3-5, *Book of Mormon*, italics added).

This formula works for any wisdom that we seek from God. Express gratitude, ask with a sincere heart following the pattern described, and receive the answer. Why does it work? Here's why:

If you think of the Lord's mercy since the beginning of time, and ponder it, you will generate a feeling of gratitude which puts you in harmony with God, and prepares you to *feel* an answer when you ask for one.

Take a moment to try to be better in tune with Him as you express gratitude for as many things as you can think of below, or ideally, in your personal journal. Remember, a genuine feeling of gratitude will begin the movement of greater blessings toward you. By law.

An Expression of Gratitude

Knowing what you know now about the Law of Vibration, isn't it easier to comprehend the miracles related in the scriptures? Does this mean that with this knowledge we can cause miracles in our own life? With the Lord's help, yes. On our own? Heaven's, no. Acknowledging our dependence on Him is an attitude of humility we must maintain throughout our life, no matter how prosperous we become. Too many people stumble onto these principles and thus prosper, then conclude that they did it on their own, only to set themselves up for a terrible fall. Stay humble and grateful, always remembering He who delivered you from bondage.

Put yourself into the right "vibration" to draw near to God, and to attract the circumstances you desire. Just as an acorn planted in the earth does not have to fight and claw the dirt to find what it needs to become a great oak, neither do we need to stress or worry about our needs (fig. 7). If we plant a good idea in our fertile mind, casting away doubt seeds and weeds, the idea cannot help but grow and become what its blueprint contains.

All that an acorn needs is drawn to it, by natural law. You will be drawn to your dominant thoughts, so *plant the idea seed in your mind, do not pull it out with your doubt, and with gratitude and emotion you can put yourself into harmonious vibration with the physical counterpart of the new idea, and draw to yourself all the elements you need in order to see the idea come true.*

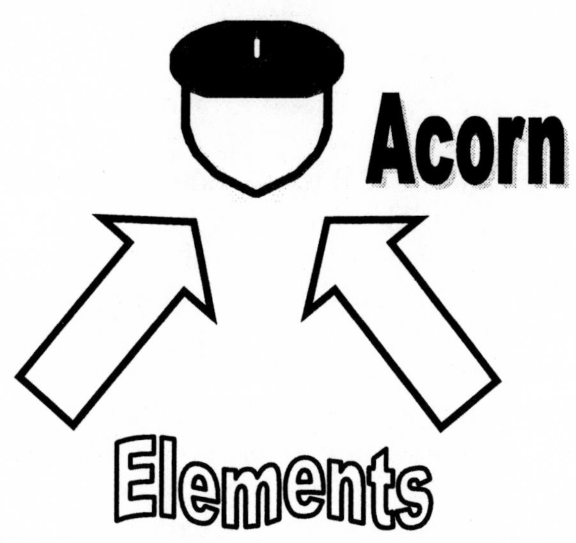

Fig. 7

Not until the image is firmly planted in our mind, does the way present itself. Too many people wait to see a way before striving for significant change in their life. That's backwards...just as the "leaf elements" and "bark molecules" will *not* begin to come together until the seed is planted and held in the ground for a sufficient amount of time. It is so clear in nature the order of events that must take place to grow a tree, but in our lives, we expect so much without patience and proper nourishment for our idea-seeds.

When my good friend Marnie decided to start dreaming a little bigger with her new understanding of the laws, she envisioned her acres of property with a fence and horses. The fence alone was going to cost a fortune but she chose to disregard the facts at hand and spend her energy building the dream. Then, one day she received a phone call and was asked if she would be willing to board some horses on her property if the horse owners were willing to put up the fence themselves.

What did Marnie do to realize her dream? She visualized it and felt grateful for it before it was a physical reality. She kept doubt, fear, impatience and frustration at bay. She believed, not having any clue how the dream would be manifest in her life.

In a book titled *Drawing on the Powers of Heaven*, Grant Von Harrison explains:

> "The thought process itself is the key to exercising faith...Your life is influenced more by your own thoughts than anything else." He continues, "Faith can be gauged to a great extent by the amount of time spent thinking about your righteous desire" (Von Harrison, Grant. 2001. *Drawing on the Powers of Heaven*, Sandy: Sounds of Zion, p. 35, used with permission).

Our thoughts have a greater effect on our circumstances than most people realize. We are not at the mercy of exterior events; we are the masters of our future. Like the rudder on a large ship, our lives are steered by our thoughts. The more we control our thoughts, the more our circumstances will actually reflect the worthy desires of our hearts. Consider this idea put another way:

> "How could a person possibly become what he is *not* thinking? Nor is any thought, when persistently entertained, too small to have its effect. The 'divinity that shapes our ends' is indeed in ourselves" (Kimball, Spencer W., 1969. *The Miracle of Forgiveness,* Salt Lake City: Bookcraft, pp. 104-105).

> *"Consider the lilies how they grow: they toil not, they spin not; and yet I say unto you, that Solomon in all his glory was not arrayed like*

> *one of these. If then God so clothe the grass, which is to day in the field, and to morrow is cast into the oven; how much more will he clothe you, O ye of little faith? And seek not what ye shall drink, neither be ye of doubtful mind...But rather seek ye the kingdom of God; and all these things shall be added unto you. Fear not, little flock; for it is your Father's good pleasure to give you the kingdom"* (Luke 12:27-32).

The Sea of Galilee Principle: So what is the principle behind making room for the new? Think of this. Have you ever really looked at a map of Israel? The Jordan River is fed from the north. It flows through the Sea of Galilee and continues south where it ends in the Dead Sea. The Dead Sea is lower than sea level, and keeps all of the water that flows to it, only releasing water through evaporation.

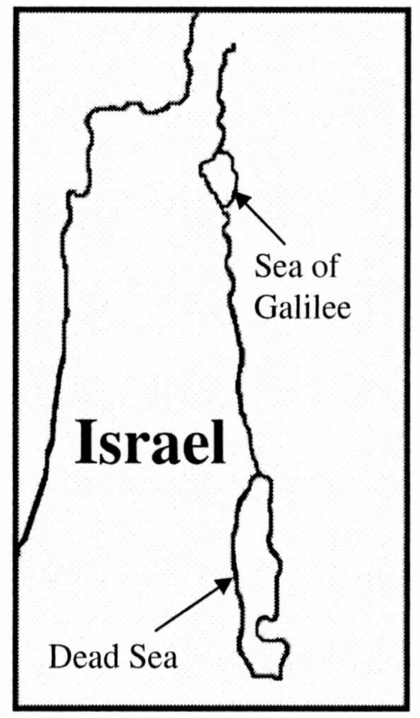

Fig. 8

Think of these two different bodies of water as two different kinds of people that we can be.

Sea of Galilee: Excellent climate, fertile, produces large crops, abundant fisheries, great source of wealth, large export trade, only approximately 85 miles square (relatively small), 680 feet below sea level, *place where Christ performed miracles.*

Sea of Galilee Personified: Cheerful disposition (excellent climate), productive, prosperous, makes significant contribution, humble (relatively 'small'), a life where Christ can perform miracles.

Dead Sea: Hot climate, infertile, approximately 500 miles square (relatively large and impressive), no outlets except for evaporation, minerals accumulate and cause extreme bitterness in the water, 1290 ft below sea level, *place of God's judgment on Sodom, Gomorrah, Admah, Zeboim, and Zoar or Bela (see Genesis 19).*

Dead Sea Personified: Not so pleasant disposition, (hot climate) fails to nourish and grow good "seeds", may *seem* great and significant, but actually operates on a "lower" plane in many ways than a humble person (approximately 600 feet deeper below sea level than Galilee). Hoards what it receives (no outlets) and ends up losing anyway. Anything that *does* remain lends to unhappiness and dissatisfaction (mineral deposits rendering the land sterile), a life in danger of God's judgement.

Same water, same source of blessings, but handling the "blessing" differently. For Christians, this metaphor is especially meaningful because Christ is so often referred to as the *Living Water*.

Are we letting blessings flow *through* us, bringing us even greater abundance, or are we stingy and selfish, bringing us desolation? Give, and make room for more! You will be reminded of this principle when we discuss the bonus Vacuum Law of Prosperity at the end of the book.

The next chapter will teach you about the Law of Polarity, which is **what you will need to know when unforeseen things happen to thwart your plan for prosperity (which they will).**

LESSON 4:

LAW OF POLARITY

In the last chapter, I mentioned that *something* would get in the way to thwart your plans. Here, we will talk about just *how* to think when that happens. I hope by now you see the importance of guiding your thoughts.... It is no less important when you are faced with opposition—in fact, it is *most* important to do when you *are* faced with opposition. You will find that how you should think during the challenging times isn't all that difficult. It actually feels good because with the following information, you will be able to be at peace in affliction, and also *know* that how you are thinking is the exact *right* way to think!

The Law of Polarity states that everything, and I mean *everything* of consequence, has an opposite. It's a *law*. You can't fall six feet down from being only four feet up. You can't turn left without coming from the right. "Yes" only exists because "No" does too; otherwise it would be meaningless.

Speaking of "meaningless," did you know you can't poke your eye out? You can poke it in, but you can't poke it out. I suppose you could reach up your nose and poke it out... (Right, Ken?)

The point is, (no pun intended) that there is no such thing as "in" if there were no "out." These are all opposites. Good, bad. Dark, light. Male, female. Each one is meaningless without the other.

It has been said in this way:

> "The Divine Shepherd has a message of hope, strength, and deliverance for all. If there were no night, we would not appreciate the day, nor could we see the stars and the vastness of the heavens. We must partake of the bitter with the sweet. There is a divine purpose in the adversities we encounter every day. They prepare, they purge, they purify, and thus they bless" (Faust, James E. 1979. The Refiner's Fire. *Ensign,* May).

It is important to realize that the experiences that we call unfortunate are, in every case, good for us. If they are not the more obvious "feel good" blessing, they are character building experiences. We'll get through our trials. If we don't give up, we'll conquer and learn important lessons with the help of the Lord, but we have to keep our eyes on the prize in order to benefit from tragedies and hardships. Just knowing that opposition is a natural part of our life experience can help us deal with disappointments.

> *"For it must needs be, that there is an opposition in all things. If not so, my first-born in the wilderness, righteousness could not be brought to pass, neither wickedness, neither holiness nor misery, neither good nor bad. Wherefore, all things must needs be a compound in one"* (1 Nephi 2:11, *Book of Mormon*).

The Law of Polarity also declares that everything has an opposite that is of *equal degree.* In other words, if it is very, very far to walk from Los Angeles to Phoenix, then it is equally very, very far to walk from Phoenix to Los Angeles. So long as the elements of the situation remain constant, there will always be two perspectives from which to view it. In this case, the direction of travel is the only difference. It is the *same* distance both ways.

There are basic elements of any situation, but the situation itself is never fundamentally good or bad. We talked about this in Lesson 2, as we learned by the Law of Relativity that things are only good or bad relative to something else. In this lesson, we learn that things have within them both good and bad. When you experience a “bad” situation, then this Law of Polarity may assure you that there is, within it, something good.

If something is a little bit bad, then it is only a little bit good. If something is catastrophic, then there is, within it, something phenomenal!

*Opposite. **Equal** and opposite.*

Napoleon Hill, one of the most quoted authors from twentieth century self-help literature said:

> "Every adversity, every failure, and every heartache carries with it the seed of an equivalent or greater benefit” (Hill, Napoleon. 1960. *Think and Grow Rich*, New York: Faucett Crest, p. 74).

Suppose something comes along that seems insurmountable to you while you are in pursuit of your goal…

The worse it seems, the better it is, really.

I believe that's one reason why the survivors of the Martin Handcart Company from Lesson 2 were able to feel privileged to have been a part of the group. In their extremities, they became acquainted with God Himself. I don't really get more acquainted with God when I stub my toe, you know? And what greater thing could we ever achieve than to know God? I don't mean, "know *about* God," I mean, "*know* Him."

Consider the story of Gideon and the Midianites, (Judges, chapter 7). There is such a powerful lesson in this story to help you understand why obstacles are part of the process. Gideon was called to lead his army to conquer the Midianites. There were 32,000 men in his army, and the Lord told him that he had too many. (Too many?! Who wouldn't want too many?!) Do you ever look at your situation and think, "It would sure be nice if I had more going for me!" Well, read on....

The Lord told Gideon to find out who in his army was afraid to go to battle. What was he told to do with those who were afraid? They were to be sent away. (But aren't sheer numbers an advantage? *Not if the numbers bring **fear** to the fight.*) So he did, and he was left with 10,000.

Once again, the Lord said he had too many. Why? Well, the Lord knew that if they went to battle with a large army and won, that they would pat themselves on the back for conquering the foe themselves. God wanted them to know, without a doubt, that He was responsible for their victory. (God wants *your* victory, and He wants you to *know* that you couldn't have done it without Him. If the task is too easy, then when you conquer, you might think it was *your* strength alone that did the job.)

So the Lord told Gideon to take the men to the water to let them drink. Those who brought the water to their mouths with their hands he kept, those who knelt and drank directly from the body of water were sent home. How many men were left to fight the battle? Only three hundred!

Insurmountable odds. (Do you feel like the odds are against you too?) To me, water is symbolic in the scriptures for Christ. I was taught: Come unto Christ, for he is the Living Water. In our pursuit of prosperity, I felt I should do as Gideon did with the little 'thought soldiers' I have in my head...by sending the fearful ones away, and then relying on Christ, the Living Water.

By stratagem, God made Gideon victorious, in such a clever way! The men were told to surround the

Midianites at night with lamps inside their pitchers in one hand, and a trumpet in the other. Upon Gideon's signal, they shouted together, broke their pitchers and blew their trumpets. In the darkness, the groggy Midianites saw and heard all of the commotion and ended up confused, fighting against each other and fleeing away. Gideon had conquered without a single one of his men even being wounded.

Your goal will be accomplished through God, most likely in a clever way as well.

I've seen too many people give up on a goal because "things got hard." I've even heard some say that "everything went wrong…so that's a sign that it wasn't supposed to happen for me." Things *will* get hard! But that's just the evidence you need to know that the reward is just that much closer! Come on! Satan *is* opposition, and he tends to really give it all he's got right before the blessing, in hopes you'll give up. Too often, too many of us do.

> *"I would show unto the world that faith is things which are hoped for and not seen; wherefore, dispute not because ye see not, for ye receive no witness until after the trial of your faith"* (Ether 12:6, *Book of Mormon*).

Keep in mind also that even if we don't get what we desire when we want it, consider *that* opposition, and keep at it. Don't throw the laws away because something didn't happen according to your plan. Rest assured: the reward will be just that much better for your patience.

My father taught me that **God doesn't always come when you want him to, but He's never late**. You'll learn more about that in our final lesson.

Keep your thoughts focused on the desired result, in spite of the lack of evidence that it is coming. Remember, as you hold on to your focused thoughts, the formless substance is gathering to cause your idea to materialize. And when an elephant sits on you, look for the blessing that will come out of it. You don't have to know what the blessing will be. Just know that it will be just exactly what it needs to be for your good.

Trust that God knows best, and won't lead you to misery, but joy—greater than you can comprehend. As you look for the good in a bad situation, you will be preparing yourself to find and receive the good that is there. If you never look for it, you may never find it, and you could live your whole life only seeing the bad. The high achievers, those who live abundantly, make this a habit: they look for good, and more good comes.

Your desired results always follow a trial of your faith. It is a test. What a thrill it is to pass the test! Pass the test by holding on to your belief and sending away the "fearful thoughts" in your mind! Draw nearer to God through the refiner's fire. The greater the challenge, the greater the reward...**by law!**

> *"My brethren, count it all joy when ye fall into divers temptations; Knowing this, that the trying of your faith worketh patience"* (James 1:2-3).

It's *all* good. All things will work together for your good. It might seem bad, but know that by this Law of Polarity, it is *good*, too. Think about that part of it, and what you desire will continue toward you.

> *"And if thou shouldst be cast into the pit, or into the hands of murderers, and the sentence of death passes upon thee; if thou be cast into the deep; if the billowing surge conspire against thee; if fierce winds become thine enemy; if the heavens gather blackness, and all the elements combine to hedge up the way; and above all, if the very jaws of hell shall*

> *gape open the mouth wide after thee, know thou,...that all these things shall give thee experience, and shall be for thy good"* (Doctrine and Covenants 122:7).

...if the sheriff comes after thee and takes thine house from thee, or if the utility company threatens to shut off thy water...or if thou conkest thy head on the corner of thy cupboard...

It's all just part of the mortal experience. Do all you can do and trust that whatever happens is for your good.

So-called failure isn't fatal. Take courage and face your problems head on. Do not run from creditors, have the integrity to contact them *first* if there is a problem. Don't wait for *them* to be the ones to announce there is a delinquency. Integrity is foundational to these ideas. You must be committed to honesty in all your dealings with your fellow man. God has provided a way for us to keep all of the commandments, and honesty is something we must take seriously. So be sure to live that law *now*, in your present circumstances. Your financial life will improve; you will find the abundance you seek. But never compromise your integrity in the pursuit, or it will all come falling down. Live by LAW. It will set you free.

(An interesting piece of information that I hadn't realized before: I've played with Legos for more than thirty years and never knew what the name meant until I looked up the company to provide trademark credit for this book. Did you know that Lego comes from the Danish words "Leg Godt", which means "Play well"? In Latin it means "I put together". Both phrases beautifully embody the principles of building a better life on a creative plane.)

LESSON 5:

LAW OF RHYTHM

Remember when we discussed that everything vibrates? The world is in an "ocean of motion." I like that phrase; it's another one I adopted from Bob Proctor. Well, for this lesson, I'd like you to think about the world, as that "ocean of motion." But instead of picturing a buzzing and blurry collection of atoms and molecules bumping around all over the place, imagine the movement of things as being smooth and peaceful. Like an ocean. The tide rises and falls. The waves come in and they go out. Microscopically, the elements *are* chaotically bumping around all over the place, but zoom out, and you'll see **rhythm**.

I studied Mathematics in college. As a part of my studies, I was able to take a brief look at a recently discovered phenomenon that the scientists call "Chaos." James Gleick wrote an excellent book on the subject. But it doesn't sound all that scientific, does it? Sounds like my house, with six little ones running around underfoot. But it *is* fascinating to study. The experts have looked at things in nature, things that seem random or things that seem disorderly, and have been discovering patterns that were not obvious before. They have taken mammal population data and where results seemed erratic, with computer imaging, they have graphed the data, and by zooming *way, way* out, they see patterns that they had never noticed before. By dropping an ink droplet in water, they have seen quantifiable similarities between the shapes it creates as it falls, and the physical characteristics of a jellyfish. The paths of lightning, the air currents, all of these natural, unpredictable behaviors have more "to them" than we have understood.

My favorite example of patterns in nature is captured in a scientist's illustration of how a shoreline looks from different perspectives:

Suppose a man is asked to measure the length of Great Britain's shoreline. He could take a yardstick and walk it off and then count the number times the yardstick was placed along the shoreline. But if he took a ruler, and did the same thing, he would get a different overall length. This is because the yardstick cannot account for the ins and outs of the shoreline that occur within the space of the yard, the way the ruler can. The ruler would be responsible for measuring a lengthier shoreline.

Again, he would end up with an entirely different measurement by using a smaller unit, because it would account for the jagged ins and outs that could not be measured with a ruler.

Now if he were to repeat this process, measuring with shorter and shorter units until he was finally negotiating each pebble, or grain of sand, the measured length of the shoreline would be nearly at its longest. What's my point? Hang in there, it's coming....

I remember a song from my childhood, something about "That's about the size, **where you put your eyes**, that's about the size...of...it!" In other words, how big it is depends on a point of view.

As for the shoreline, the "ins and outs" exist at *each* level of measurement. Right? But no matter what the unit of measurement, the resulting waterline would still consist of ins and outs. Pictorially, the jagged edges are just as jagged from 30 miles off the ground as they are from 15 miles, 10 feet, 2 inches, etc. This is *fractal geometry*. It's really quite amazing, and it's the stuff that has made computer-generated images so realistic.

Interestingly enough, this fractal geometry parallels our own experiences. Our experiences have a common theme no matter how we look at them: our "shoreline" is a timeline....

Our "ins and outs" are ups and downs. We have prosperous years and we have challenging years. These years are made up of prosperous *months* and challenging months. These months are made up of prosperous *days* and challenging days. These days are made up of *moments* worth celebrating, and moments that we just can't seem to handle.

I believe that God uses nature to teach us about life and ourselves. His lessons for us are everywhere in the world around us. **What do we learn from this lesson? We learn that, by law, we are guaranteed better times ahead.**

If we're on a down, we can *expect* an up! Start expecting it! If it's been a bad year, start looking forward to the good year coming! If it's been a bad day, get excited about the good one just around the corner. This law is our reason for being able to look forward with certainty to God's blessings. Maybe that's why God gave us a shoreline, so that when we look at it, if we *really* study His creation, we would actually learn ***hope*!** Is that God's message to us in a shoreline? Maybe, maybe not. Still, I know He wants us to embrace hope.

> *"The hope of the righteous shall be gladness"* (Proverbs 10:28).
>
> *"But if we hope for that we see not, then do we with patience wait for it"* (Romans 8:25).
>
> *"[Be] rejoicing in hope; patient in tribulation; continuing instant in prayer"* (Romans 12:12).

So, the **Law of Rhythm states that nature's movements are cyclical. There is repetition in everything.** We see this in the way the planets move, in the seasons, in the tide, and even in our personal circumstances. We have our own sort of biorhythm. We feel good, we feel bad. We experience joy, and sadness, over and over throughout our life.

Because of the Law of Polarity we know why these experiences are important. The sad times give meaning to the happy times. Without them, we wouldn't know what happiness was. Ecclesiastes chapter 3 teaches that there is a season for everything, and by the mere use of the word "season," we deduce that the times to weep and laugh are cyclical. The times to get and the times to lose are also going to be repeated, just as the seasons repeat.

It does not say, "To every thing, there is a moment!" Neither does it say, "To every thing, there is permanence." It says, "To every thing, there is a *season*."

I try to use my knowledge of this law to my advantage. When I'm overcome with despair, I remember that I can count on an upturn of events. I begin to look for evidence of it. You may want to review the Law of Perpetual Transmutation to see why *doing this will literally bring the upswing sooner.*

So, if things are good, do we have to expect things to go bad, by law? No, you'd be shooting yourself in the foot to entertain such thoughts. This is an example of one of those times I said to choose wisely the law, or "tool" in your toolbox. Don't be thinking about the "friction" on your "satellite" during "re-entry" if you have no intention or desire of having it re-enter. *Choose your thoughts. Intentionally exercise your free agency to choose your thoughts. It will pay you great dividends.*

Here's what you do instead:

Remember the Law of Polarity by which we know that even the worst circumstances are actually fabulous. There you go! That's the tool you must summon.

Not satisfied? Okay, skeptics; approach it this way: Picture a horizontal wavy line, (fig. 9). Up and down, up and down. Some people look at life this way. They are up, so they expect things will eventually go down. "This feeling can't last forever." **Step aside, friends**. They're attracting exactly what they expect.

On the other hand, there are people that strive for better times, and when they experience some, they get comfortable there and level out. Eventually they become dissatisfied with their circumstances, and what was once wonderful becomes commonplace. They may feel low. But it isn't because they *are* low; it is because their divine nature beckons them to seek even better circumstances. However, to them, they'll be feeling the Law of Rhythm in action. They'll feel like they are on a low, and have come down from a "high." But from God's perspective, I believe it looks more like *eternal progression,* higher levels of awareness, continual learning, continual growth, and approaching their potential. *That horizontal wavy line can be rotated just forty-five degrees, and the ups and downs* ***instead*** *become...a stairway,* (fig. 10). True happiness comes from the feeling that our soul is expanding, that we are learning and applying something new that brings us closer to God.

Fig. 9

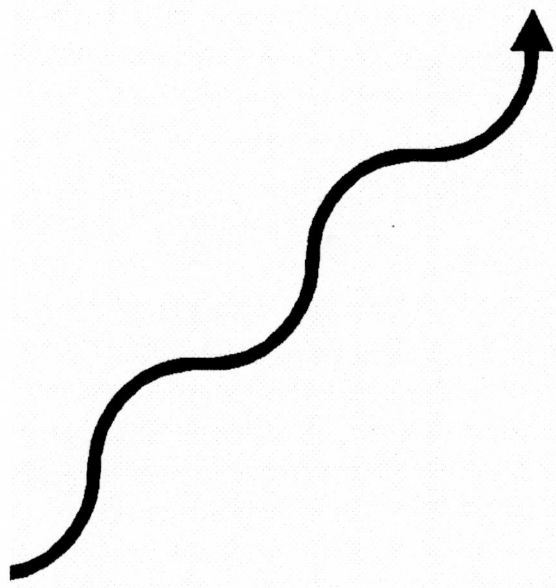

Fig. 10

Those who expect and seek for good things will experience this kind of growth, while those who don't exercise their faith to attract good things will only experience the ups and downs of going nowhere, or worse, a gradual decline.

So, when you are down, expect to go up. When you are up, expect that one day your "up" won't be enough to keep you happy and it will feel like a down. It's all good. Look forward to feeling better, but you don't have to force it to happen. Nature provides; it will happen all on its own. *Calm down* and refuse to worry about bad things that haven't happened, and which may *never* happen. "*Be still, and know that I am God*" (Psalms 46:10), is good advice when you are on a "down."

A beautiful merging of the Laws of Relativity, Rhythm, and Polarity: Why can't we just aim high and make a steady upward climb? The fact is that we wouldn't want to. Something inside of us longs for the natural rhythms of life. It is what makes us *feel*.

Think of a baby. You might hold him gently with his head on your shoulder, and he might be sleepy, but he is better comforted with you in the rocking chair than on the sofa. As he drifts off to sleep, the rhythmic pressure assures him you are still there. Sometimes the same goal can be accomplished by a gentle patting on the back, slow and rhythmic, until he is finally asleep.

Rhythm is soothing. Rhythm is life. Too much of the same thing makes us restless. We need change to feel alive. Sometimes the "downs" in life are exactly what we need to appreciate and *feel* the "highs." And thanks to the Law of Relativity from

Chapter 2, and the Law of Polarity from Chapter 4, even the "downs" can bring us joy.

Visualize this: You are a passenger getting into a car. Close your eyes. I want you to pay attention to the laws of physics that are affecting your body. Oh, well…just *pretend* your eyes are closed. Here we go:

The engine is running and you feel the gentle vibration. It begins to go in reverse. You feel that. Your eyes are closed and you still know what is happening because you feel it. You stop briefly, and you feel that too. Then it is put into drive and you are on your way. You feel the acceleration, from 0 to 25 and on up to 65 miles per hour. It sort of sucks you into the back of your chair. But then the pressure isn't so strong anymore. In fact, it feels like nothing is going on. It feels just like it did before you put it in reverse in the first place. You don't feel anything. Have you stopped? No, you're just traveling at a constant speed.

Whoa! All of a sudden you are thrown forward, and if you didn't know any better, you might have thought you were going backwards. But you weren't. Rather, the brakes were applied to avoid hitting something in the way. You only went from

65 mph to 50 mph. You went from feeling nothing to feeling like you are going in reverse.

Pretty soon you feel nothing again. The car has leveled out at 50 mph because it feels safer. Oh, wait, here's a new kind of feeling...you are somewhat thrown to the side. So far you have only felt forward, backward, and nothing. But now you know what a change of path feels like. You have turned a corner.

This analogy could go on and on. This is life. Any kind of change is going to make you *feel* something. Sometimes what you feel can be deceiving. Make sure you are headed in the right direction. If you are headed in the wrong direction, make a turn. You will *feel* the change. It might initially be uncomfortable, but it will bring you joy. Most importantly, make your ultimate direction *onward and upward*!

After you've climbed a little, take notice if you stop feeling the joy that came from the climb. When you do, it is time to reach a little higher. An upward climb draws you securely back into your cushion, which feels much better than a sudden drop that brings your gut into your throat, or even the feeling that you're not going anywhere. Stagnation is miserable because there is absence of progression.

To *feel* requires change. To feel pure joy, make a change to a more lawful way of living. We all can do better in one area of our life or another. Commit to a life of upward climbing. When you level out, whether or not you are still moving forward, in order to *feel* again, you'll need to climb again.

We're all seeking to *feel* more alive, to *feel* more peace, and to *feel* more happiness. Some turn to drug abuse or immorality because these things cause strong, but deceptive feelings. To surrender to these temptations generates a powerful, but temporary imitation of true happiness.

Such feelings are counterfeit and *will not last*; in fact, they can leave a person craving more of the same until they become completely enslaved by the addiction.

To do nothing more than *experiment* with such vices can even be enough to keep a person from having enough patience, diligence, and discipline to ever discover the secrets of achieving deeply satisfying, *real and lasting joy.*

In fact, to indulge in these forged thrills actually violates not only spiritual law, but natural law as well. A person does not have to believe in God to suffer the consequences attached to the breaking of these natural laws. A person physical makeup is affected, and he or she will eventually suffer not just any "low," but a "low" that is lower than the last "low." The kind of punishment he/she will receive in the hereafter depends on the degree of his/her understanding of the law before he/she decided to violate it. Irregardless, the natural, short term consequences will always follow, no matter how much a person knows about God.

Such natural consequences can be evidence alone that the induced thrill was a counterfeit to the much stronger, more satisfying, longer lasting genuine version God provides those who pay the price to live by law. Contrary to the ad campaigns of modern society, "*Wickedness never was happiness*" (Alma 41:10, *Book of Mormon*).

Remember that living in harmony with natural law will bring us the greatest joys and the most long-lasting happiness possible. To violate these laws will *always* bring pain and misery. By law, it will. Sooner or later...you can count on it. Not because the Lord delights in punishing us, but because the consequences are simply spontaneous and natural, like the three year-old's reaction to the 'thieving' baby.

If you've found yourself in this kind of trap, you can get out. It will probably require outside help from your religious leader and/or a professional. Since the view from inside the trap is cloudy, it is hard if not impossible to see your way out without a guide. In fact, from inside, one may not even realize there are clouds that need clearing.

We will continue to attract to us the same situations again and again because of the "vibration" we are in with our darker thoughts and feelings. To pull out is often like trying to climb out of a pit of molasses. But it is possible. It all begins with our thoughts. If our thoughts disappoint us, then we can subject ourselves to someone else's purer thoughts by choosing purer music, purer books, and purer movies and television programs.

It might take a while to start feeling *true joy*, because of the desensitization that comes from Satan's counterfeits. It will definitely require a lot of uplifting input into our minds to drown out the darker thoughts that very well may be dominant.

We need to put ourselves in good environments, and choose good friends. We will not feel comfortable there initially, because our personal, subconscious "vibration" might not be in harmony with the better environment, but good friends will help elevate our thoughts so that our inner state will eventually feel right at home. This is one reason why we must strive for pure thoughts, so that we will feel at home to live with our Father in Heaven in the next life. How could a person so out of harmony with His laws ever be comfortable in His presence? He wants you and me to return to Him, and will help us prepare for that reunion if we strive to live His teachings. The process of preparing ourselves cannot be accomplished on a moment's notice; it takes time, and we shouldn't procrastinate getting started.

What else will we need to do if we are trapped in addictive and destructive behaviors? We will need to be cautious of the kinds of music we listen to, and the kinds of shows we watch. It takes time, but the change surely comes. Even though we cannot see our fingernail growing, we know that it is because we need to trim it once in a while. We might not see our personal growth, but in time we will look back and be grateful that we made a lot of good little choices along the way. For "by small and simple things are great things brought to pass" (Alma 37:6, *Book of Mormon*).

So let's seek the natural "highs," the highs that come from living an honorable life. Serve others. Do good to those who hate you. Exercise your faith in

God. Live a disciplined life. Believe. No temporary unlawful thrill can ever match the exhilaration of diligent effort toward striving to live more like the Savior. The happiness He promises is long lasting. Stay away from Satan's counterfeits.

Since I'm not perfect, I've had to employ this counsel in my life, too. I expect I'll need to do so for as long as I live, as would anybody. Still, I can testify that to submit to the will of the Lord brings profound peace and joy. It's *so* worth the effort to strive to live the disciplined life.

Keep in mind that the Law of Rhythm guarantees that we *will* feel ups and downs. But as we learn to live "by law," we can ensure that our "lows" are only the absence of a "high." This keeps us climbing.

Take inventory: Where are you today? Are you on a "high" or "low" or feeling sort of "level?" What is one thing you could do to help yourself feel some pure joy?

____

____

____

In the first five lessons we discussed quite deeply how our thoughts affect our circumstances. This lesson leads us well into our next lesson where we will discuss **the law that helps us understand what our *actions* are doing to our results.**

LESSON 6:

LAW OF CAUSE AND EFFECT

This is probably more familiar territory to many of us. In essence, this is the Law of the Harvest, or The Golden Rule, or the New Law that Christ presented during his earthly ministry.

Hopefully, this discussion will help us see it as more than just a "good idea" to be genuinely kind to people. It is more than just a good idea, it is a **law** that we will either follow, or break ourselves against. We have to remember that by our rigid definition of law, there is no escaping the consequences. That is good news, and bad news, depending on how we choose to live this law.

The Law of Cause and Effect states that every cause has an effect, and every effect has a cause. Nothing happens by chance.

Everything that happens in the universe happens as a result of a law. There is order in everything. Nothing is unpredictable to God. Understand, however, that although He knows all things, His knowledge does not take away our free agency. That is another law that He abides perfectly: to give us our freedom to make choices. But He *can* know with certainty what will happen as we make our choices. This is because of the Law of Cause and Effect.

On the next page is a cartoon which illustrates this, and was derived from something I stumbled onto years ago. I've tried to find the original, but have been unsuccessful. I couldn't remember where I had seen it before, or who had created it in the first place. (If anyone knows who came up with this perfectly relevant cartoon, I hope they'll let me know so I can give proper credit and perhaps show the original in future editions of this book.)

"Let's just go inside and see what happens..."

Isn't this a perfect illustration of the Law of Cause and Effect? How easy is it to predict the outcome of this situation? We don't have to be God to have a pretty good idea what's going to happen.

When I was a senior in high school, my AP English teacher put me on the spot about some of my personal religious beliefs. I was the only member of my church in the room, and very possibly the only Christian there, too, since I was in a primarily Jewish community. As nervous as I was, I tried to not let my fears of being different overcome me.

One of the things on which he challenged me was, "Does God know how we're going to turn out?" "Yes, because He is all-knowing." "Then it's pretty much already decided where we'll end up? So we're predestined." "No, He knows where we'll end up, but it's still within our control." "How can it be within our control if He knows the outcome already?" "He knows us well enough to know the kinds of choices we will make, like parents who can predict the behavior of their child based on the child's nature."

My teacher never seemed quite satisfied, and I was a little disappointed in what seemed to be a weak explanation. I didn't take the confrontation personally, since I'm sure he was simply trying to challenge my critical thinking skills.

I've thought about that conversation many times since, and after learning about this Law of Cause and Effect, I can see most clearly how God can know our future. Our future should be just as predictable to ourselves based on the choices we make and the "vibration" we keep ourselves in. Can we change the outcome? Yes, if we consciously make choices which will change our vibration, and decisions different than the ones we usually make. Making a course correction requires a concerted effort...just like your automobile will not turn a corner without you turning the steering wheel.

Does God know if we will make the necessary changes or not? He's all knowing...but part of this test in life is not to prove to *God* that we are fit for His kingdom, but by making right choices, we prove to *ourselves* that we were willing to follow His plan for us. We must go through this test so that in the end ***we*** will know His judgments are just.

Newton's Third Law: We've discussed much about the principles contained in this book in terms of basic Chemistry, Physics, and even Geology. Like I said, I believe God uses the world around us to teach us lessons. This Law of Cause and Effect is no different. For this lesson, I want to bring up Newton's third law. As stated in the chapter titled Newton's Laws of Motion from the Addison Wesley's 1988 edition of *University Physics* by Sears, Zemansky, and Young:

> *"To every action, there is always opposed an equal reaction; or, the mutual actions of two bodies upon each other are always equal, and directed to contrary parts."*

In my words, "Every action has a reaction that is equal and opposite; meaning, an action *away* from you brings a reaction *towards* you which is similar in nature."

When you take a step toward the thing you desire, the thing you desire takes a step toward you.

James 4:8 shows us one wonderful way we may apply this law in our lives:

> *"Draw nigh unto God and He will draw nigh unto you."*

Thinking about this law helps me believe that I only have to go half as far as I thought I might, because the thing I desire meets me in the middle.

Do you want something good? Move in a good direction, and good things will begin to move toward you. If you plant a carrot seed, a carrot will come to you. If you plant a weed, you'll get a weed. Galatians 6:7 states:

> "*Whatsoever a man soweth, that shall he also reap.*"

Newton talks about "two bodies." For the purposes of this lesson, let's think about the two bodies as being

1) you, and
2) the formless substance.

Why? Because if you think about this law in terms of 1) you, and 2) another person, then the law seems to be inconsistent at times. Have you noticed, if you serve someone, he or she may or may not serve you back? But if you serve someone, then you are putting "good" out into the universe, and by law, "good" will be returned to you...from the universe. That is why you don't need to be concerned with the immediate reaction you get from someone you serve.

A Powerful Illustration of the Law of Cause and Effect: The following story has been told and retold in a variety of ways. I don't know where the idea originated, but it so perfectly serves as an illustration of this law that I'd like to summarize it again here:

A man who had just lost his job was driving down an old two-lane country road in his beat up car when he saw a nice, new Cadillac pulled over onto the shoulder. He stopped to see what was wrong, and an old woman explained that she had a flat tire and didn't know what to do. The man introduced himself as Joe and graciously changed the tire. When he was done, the old woman tried to pay him for his services.

Smiling, the man refused, explaining that someone had helped him once before and that if she wants to pay him back, she should simply pass on the goodwill to someone else.

The old woman was grateful and deeply touched by his unselfish gesture of kindness. Thanking him, she drove away. She thought about what he had done and with a tender feeling in her heart she pulled into a coffee shop to enjoy some hot chocolate.

The waitress who served her was clearly nine months pregnant, and her smile could not hide the weariness she felt. Still, never a complaint escaped her lips.

Thinking again of Joe, it didn't take long for the old woman to decide how she would pass along the kindness as promised. When it came time to pay the bill, the old woman handed the waitress a hundred dollar bill. With a smile, the waitress said, "I'll be back with your change..."

While the young woman was gone, the old woman slipped away. Bringing the change back to the table, the young expectant mother looked for the old woman but only found a note which said, "Keep the change, a gift for your baby." Tears filled her eyes as she looked out the window just in time to see the elderly lady drive away.

Later that night, the expectant mother returned to her home where her husband was waiting. She approached him from behind the couch and tenderly put her arms around his shoulders. She showed him the woman's gift and said, "Everything is going to be all right... I love you, *Joe*."

Our actions are like perfectly obedient boomerangs: whatever we send out will return to us, BY LAW.

Remember, you don't have to know where your needed blessings will come from. Just know that they will. Joe could have accepted the money, and saved some time in the transaction process. She was a generous woman; perhaps the hundred dollars would have been his, right from the start. But there's a message in this principle. If we immediately see the results of our kindness, then it is easy to take the credit. If we are kind and generous, without expectation of a reward, then it is the Lord's delight to involve as many people in the blessing as possible, and who can help but give Him the glory when the blessing comes back from someplace unexpected? In this story, it only required two transactions for the blessing to come back to Joe. In our life, it might take two, and then it might take twenty...but it *will* come.

Let this 6th law be a reminder to "love one another" as the New Testament tells us that Christ has loved us. Know that, by this law, you cannot do something good, and miss the reward. By the same token, you cannot be stingy, rude, or cheat someone without an equal reaction that will come back to bite you. You cannot be selfish, or concerned with worldly acclaim, without these unworthy motives securing your decline. Your thoughts have power to produce the things you need, but always maintain gospel principles in your efforts to obtain them.

Matthew 6:4 says:

> *"That thine alms may be in secret: and thy Father which seeth in secret himself shall reward thee openly."*

Seek abundance for the purpose of doing good: for helping others, for providing the necessities for your family, for paying all of your obligations in a timely and honest way.

Do not seek abundance for impressing people, or for proving anything to your neighbors. We have to watch that the things we do with our money are good things. This law must remind us that we *will be caught* if our actions are unworthy. Do not do good deeds in hopes that people will know you did and be impressed with you.

Matthew 6:19-20 teaches us:

> *"Lay not up for yourselves treasures upon earth, where moth and rust doth corrupt, and where thieves break through and steal: But lay up for yourselves treasures in heaven, where neither moth nor rust doth corrupt, and where thieves do not break through nor steal."*

Of course it is *good* to seek riches, if the riches are used to help us keep His commandments more perfectly.

How abundantly has the Lord blessed you already? Are you striving to multiply what He has given you, as was taught in the Parable of the Talents? (See Matthew 25.) Or are you only in maintenance mode? Hopefully you aren't just hanging on to your talents (an ancient form of money), with a fear of losing them. As taught in Matthew, he who hides his talent will eventually lose it altogether. So, we should seek an increase. Besides, we cannot offer financial relief to the needy if our own purse is empty.

To do good things with money is to lay up for yourself treasures in heaven. Pay ten percent of your income to tithing. Put the Lord first and there will be a way for your own needs to be met. Malachi 3:10 teaches:

> *"Bring ye all the tithes into the storehouse, that there may be meat in mine house, and prove me now herewith, saith the Lord of hosts, if I will not open you the windows of heaven, and pour you out a blessing, that there shall not be room enough to receive it."*

Forget about LUCK. Think of L.U.C.K. as **L**iving **U**nder **C**orrect **K**nowledge. Live by law, and you are lucky. People will start to say about you, "Everything just seems to come her way." Or, "He is always so lucky."

LUCK is
Living **U**nder **C**orrect **K**nowledge

Our final lesson in this book will address the "timing" concern. **When will I see the fruits of my thoughts and my labor? How long do I need to believe?**

LESSON 7:

LAW OF GENDER AND GESTATION

Throughout these lessons we have been looking at the way our natural world operates, and we have been discovering parallels that help us understand how we can shape our circumstances. This final lesson does the same.

The Law of Gender states that in all of creation there is male and female in every kind. For life to perpetuate there must be one to plant the seed, and one to grow and nourish the seed. In some cases, one creature accomplishes both tasks.

So for an idea-seed to be created and then manifest in the physical world, there must be an idea planter and an idea grower. Your mind is the recipient of innumerable idea seeds. The media is trying to plant a field of ideas to get you to move into a vibration that is in harmony with their products. The adversary is trying to sell you a lifestyle through other media that will only bring you misery. Your own genetics may be responsible for faulty thinking if you permit. So long as you let these influences plant their varieties, your results will be in their control, not yours.

You may plant your own idea seeds. Choose good seeds by exposing yourself to good input on purpose. Plant good seeds by creating a new, prosperous idea for your life. You have the power to create a picture in your mind that is completely original.

> "Every thought seed sown or allowed to fall into the mind, and to take root there, produces its own, blossoming sooner or later into act, and bearing its own fruitage of opportunity and circumstance. Good thoughts bear good fruit, bad thoughts bad fruit" (Allen, 16).

The Law of Gestation states that every seed has an incubation period. In other words, once a seed is placed in the right environment, it begins to develop and reaches maturity after a certain period of time. Farmers know just how long it takes for a pumpkin seed to turn into a pumpkin. They know just how long to wait before they should pull up the radishes. They don't panic when their strawberries are green instead of red; they know that the process just isn't finished yet.

The same Law applies to the animal kingdom. The gestation period is approximately forty weeks for a human, fifty-two for an elephant, two for a mouse.

Ideas are seeds, too. Held in your mind and nourished there, they grow, mature, and eventually bear fruit. For a reminder of that principle, review Lesson 1, the Law of Perpetual Transmutation. Every idea also has a gestation, or incubation period. But we don't know what it is. I do know that the greater the intensity of our seeking, the sooner we find. The degree of faith we have also has an effect. *Both of these elements are within our control.*

We can increase the intensity of our seeking. We can pray more fervently. We can fast (for example, try skipping food and water for two meals, replacing eating with meditation). We can focus our efforts. Like sunlight and a magnifying glass, our focused thoughts can be dramatically effective.

We can increase our faith through study, and obedience. All of these things help us draw on the powers of heaven to our benefit. They put us in a vibration that is in closer harmony to God, and it is within reason to believe that the closer we are to the Source of all blessings, the more blessed we will be.

Every thing has an appointed time. Things come in waves. The economy is like that. But does that mean that what you seek will come in its appointed time, regardless of your behavior? Not necessarily. All that you need is already all around you, so while you wait for it, you must be preparing yourself. Prepare *yourself* to receive. By faith, it comes. By action, you receive it.

The sun comes and goes every twenty-four hours. If you are in a dark box, and want sunlight, then you know that it already exists and will come to you. But if you do not get out or open the lid, then when it comes, you will not be able to receive it. Perhaps the length of time you must wait depends on when you finally take affirmative action.

If you come out of your box at midnight or noon it won't matter, the sun will shine on you in time.

Remember, all we need is already in the universe all around us. By applying these principles from the last six lessons, we are opening the lid on the box, and preparing ourselves to receive the blessing. The length of time we must wait depends to some degree on what time of day, so to speak, we remove the lid. It may be a little different for everyone, but it *will* come, just as we can depend on a sunrise. We are putting *ourselves* in the right vibration to receive what we desire.

(A word about marriage to my single readers: Are you looking for the right one? *BE* the kind of person you seek, and the right one will be naturally drawn to you at the right time. If you continue to attract the kinds of people you don't want, you must change *your* vibration by changing your thoughts. Try to think the way the kind of person you want would think. If you want a spiritual companion, you must be spiritually minded. If you want a health-conscious companion, you must be health conscious first. But remember, your vibration does not change by your thoughts alone, but by turning those thoughts over to your subconscious mind through strong emotional feelings. In other words, you must take time to imagine being with the kind of person you dream of, and feel the joy of it *now.* Feel the gratitude you expect to feel; imagine the prayer of gratitude you would expect to utter on the day of your wedding.)

We Can be So Stubborn, Can't We? Elements in nature are predictable because they are 100%

obedient to God's laws. We, on the other hand, are more stubborn. We have free agency to choose what we will become. We have within us a blueprint, a pattern plan, for success, but we have the ability to change it by our thoughts. As we dream of becoming the best we can be, we are actually growing toward that end. With negative self-talk, we begin to grow toward a less glorious end. God teaches us by his laws how to reach our highest potential. If only we could be as obedient to laws as are the elements.

The gestation period for our ideas is set, and is finite. If we do our part, the reward will come quicker, because we are preparing ourselves for the very next 'sunrise.'

However, our ideas will never come faster than the period of time they take to mature. I heard it said that just because the baby doesn't come when you expect it to, it doesn't mean you aren't still pregnant. A pregnant woman can depend on the fact that she will not be pregnant forever. (Oh thank heavens for that!) Just as we don't always understand the reason that the baby comes a little sooner than expected or a little later than expected...we don't have to know the exact date that our idea will be delivered.

Think big! Create a new idea for your life that is so big it scares you! A big miracle is no more difficult for God to perform than a small one. It has been said and quoted so many times that I do not know who said it first, "Make no small plans, for they have not the magic to stir men's souls." And the beautiful thing is that it doesn't take twice as long to accomplish twice as much. *If a woman is pregnant with twins, she does not have to wait eighteen months, in fact she will probably deliver a month sooner than a mother carrying one child.*

Stop and consider the possible lesson in *that* law of nature! Could God be telling you that you can do more than you ever thought possible? It doesn't take twice as much effort to accomplish twice as much! It doesn't take twice as long to earn twice as much! If it takes one year to earn what you do, then by this principle you can earn twice as much in *less than one year*.

DON'T limit your results by deciding how long something should take. Just be at peace knowing it is truly coming. A baby giraffe takes longer to develop than a baby whale by about two months! You don't have to know when; you just have to know that it *will* come.

We don't manage the creative process. I don't know how to make an ear, but I made one. I've made twelve ears actually.

Is it blasphemous to say "I made an ear" if I know that God creates the children (and their ears, of course) and I'm just a co-creator? By the same token, I know I shouldn't take credit for the ideas I have that actually reach maturity and come into reality. Granted, I may have planted the idea, and held on to it, believing it would come, but nature, or God, did the rest.

For a couple who has struggled to conceive or a woman who has struggled to carry a baby full-term, it is not always an easy thing to believe that a baby will come. Their experience has affected their ability to maintain a child-like faith that the thing they desire will undoubtedly be realized.

In the same way, we may struggle to believe that our dreams of *any* kind will come true if we have had previous dreams shattered and abandoned. Somehow we have to muster the same kind of childlike faith that a first-time mother has who's never had any *reason* to doubt.

Understanding the laws has somehow given me just what I needed to turn back the clock and have the faith of a child.

So, suppose a woman has successfully conceived, but then the baby doesn't come as planned. Suppose it miscarries. She must trust that the reason for it is that something was wrong. She will need to trust that it is better to let nature interrupt the dream and allow her to simply try again.

In terms of other goals, when a dream does not come true, we do not quit trying, we plant a new idea. If a couple wants a baby, and they experience a miscarriage, do they throw away the hopes of having a baby? Do they decide that it just wasn't a good idea? No, they keep hoping, and keep trying, *just as we should keep trying with our ideas of prosperity.* If it hasn't come yet, go through these chapters and be sure you are doing YOUR part. Be sure you are applying all the laws to your advantage:

- Have your idea written down and well defined, and remember:
- You always gravitate toward your dominant thoughts.

- You can keep your thoughts positive by comparing your situation to something worse and exercising gratitude.
- You can change your vibration by changing your thoughts which can change your emotions or feelings, which control your vibration, and you are drawn to circumstances and things that are in harmonious vibration with yourself.
- There are opposites in everything: if your situation is catastrophic, then it is simultaneously wonderful. Look for the good in every situation; it's there for you to find.
- There is rhythm in nature; better times are always coming, by law. Good times don't have to indicate that bad ones are on their way. Rather, your good times will one day be unsatisfying and you will need to seek even better times. This leads us on to continual progression.
- Just as your thoughts affect your circumstances, so do your actions. Send *good* out into the universe and it will always come back to you.

If you are doing all these things, then be at peace. God does the rest. Ultimately the only thing that really matters is that we remain faithful to God, no matter what. These principles are here to help us use our agency as responsibly as possible. But God is still in charge.

Test the principles, and take note of what they do for you.

How long must you wait? You must wait as long as it takes. If it came sooner than the Law dictates, then it wouldn't be what you want. A mother-to-be may be anxious to have the baby, but she must be patient. *She doesn't want the embryo, she wants the baby*.

You don't want your idea to come half-baked. Give it time. In the meantime, work on you. Prepare yourself to receive it. Prepare yourself to be ready when it comes. Put the buckets out before the rain comes.

> "The story is told of a woman whose business was going under. She decided to pray to win the lottery. So she prayed and prayed that she'd win the lottery to save her business. But the lottery came and went and she didn't win.
>
> "After losing her business, she was in danger of losing her home. So she prayed and prayed

> to win the lottery. But the lottery came and went and she didn't win.
>
> "Then she was out on the street with her children, homeless and in the most destitute of circumstances. She prayed and pleaded, 'Lord, why didn't you help me win the lottery? I prayed and prayed, but you didn't answer me.'
>
> To which the Lord replied with a deep booming voice from heaven, '[YOU DIDN'T] BUY A TICKET'" (Marnie Pehrson. 2002. *10 Steps to Fulfilling Your Divine Destiny: A Christian Woman's Guide to Learning & Living God's Plan for Her.* Georgia: CES Business Consultants, p. 83, used with permission).

Don't misunderstand; the author of this quote and I both agree that the point is *not* that you should go buy a lottery ticket. (That would be gambling at irresponsible odds the very money the Lord has already blessed you with in an attempt to obtain wealth on the competitive plane! Whew, that's a mouthful!) The point is that you must do your part. Don't blame God for your troubles. Do all you can do, always believing.

The House Story: A couple years ago I decided to use these laws to try and get into a larger, nicer home. No, we couldn't afford one. But as a very successful businessman named Dexter Yager says, "If the dream is big enough, the facts don't count!" I didn't worry about the "how," I only focused on the "what." I didn't have anything in savings. Our credit wasn't perfect. But I literally spent a whole week in my room visualizing what it would be like to be in the larger home. I put a lot of detail in my mental picture, and I allowed myself to feel the joy and gratitude as though it were already mine. (I was changing my 'vibration'.)

I knew the house would have a runaround (something my mother had taught me was important for a family with young children—so they could chase each other and always have an escape), and a certain number of rooms, and a certain kind of roof, and other things that were important to me. I only left my thinking room to tend to my family as needed. Near the end of the week I had an idea come to me that I should go out on an errand; I can't even remember what the errand was. But as I turned a corner near my house, I saw a big truck getting ready to haul a load away from a home that had just been taken over by a bank. They let me inside, and as I looked around, it had every feature I had envisioned. I

KNEW that house would be mine. I was so confident in these principles that I knew they would accept anything I had to offer them for the purchase. I also believed that in time I'd figure out a way to come up with a down payment; after all, I had done everything I had been taught to do. I contacted the bank and put in an offer that I believed I could afford, which was probably two-thirds the value of the home.

But they declined. THEY DECLINED?? What about these principles? I had been so sure of this! What happened? That was a hard pill to swallow. But I very quickly decided that something better must be on its way, and I felt gratitude that God knew better than I did what should come of this. I was grateful to know that He is wiser than I, and trusted he knew how to bless me perfectly.

So I kept looking. Finally, another home came up on the bid list. Its description was not impressive. In fact, it appeared to be a real lousy deal. It indicated a certain square footage, and an overly inflated offer price. For being on a "repo" list, the price was ridiculous. But it was in the right area, so I went to look at it anyway.

I couldn't believe it. The square footage had been listed wrong. It was everything I wanted, AND

MORE. It had a pool, crown molding, Wainscoting, landscaping, RV parking, a shed, etc. At the time, all of these features were more than I could have expected. Coming from the lifestyle I had been accustomed to, I was extremely grateful that I was at least in a home, and not still in a run-down apartment in an undesirable part of town.

I wasn't sure about this house. It was a little "too much" for me. But I stopped by the house over and over, and tried to picture living there. Could I deserve it? Could I be comfortable there? I spent "thinking time" in the backyard under the moon there. I think the neighbors must have concluded that I had already bought it for how much I hung around. (We even hung our favorite painting of the Lion and the Lamb over the fireplace, just to see how it would look. We left it there during this whole process.)

Finally, the bid date came. Our agent humored us by submitting a very low bid, a figure I felt comfortable with. He gave us his prediction of how many tens of thousands more it would probably go for. I had spent so much time "courting" this dream that I came to want that house very badly. I became pretty emotional about it and nearly had our agent submit a higher bid, and then hope for a way to come through with our offer. But we didn't succumb to the temptation. We decided that our figure was what we could pay, and if it was going to be ours, then it would be ours. If not, then there would be something even better still.

We had to wait a few days before we would hear back on the results of the auction. In the meantime, I drove over to the house and parked in front of it again. I felt an invitation from God that said, "Just ask." I pondered the impression, and felt His Spirit confirm the invitation. So I bowed my head, closed my eyes, and said, "Dear Father, you know what is best for me. I know that if we don't get this house, then there will be something better suited to us. But I also feel your invitation. Father, I want this house, and I am asking thee now, please, let me have this blessing, according to thy will. This is my request, in the name of Jesus Christ, amen." After that, I felt calm and peaceful, and did not allow myself to worry. It was out of my hands; I had done all I could do. I "let go, and let God."

Friday morning I came home to find a message on my answering machine from my agent. With a chuckle, he said, "Well...we got it. I don't believe it, but we got it!" We cried, we celebrated, and we loved our home. We have since moved to a home that more completely meets all of our needs now that our family has grown, and we maintain gratitude for it as well.

Remembering the very first house I had seen, I felt so much gratitude that we *didn't* get it. The location wasn't nearly as good, and it wasn't nearly as attractive to me as the one we bought. The first one didn't have the upgrades and added features, either. It needed a lot of fixing up. The one we bought was amazing to us—it had gone through foreclosure because the previous owners had overextended themselves with too many home improvements and upgrades on second and third mortgages.

I feel that getting ourselves into a better home began with my learning the principles and spending all of that time visualizing and feeling. A greater understanding of the laws has strengthened my faith in God. It has helped me believe in miracles which would have been too incredible to hope for previously.

Other things started to come our way that were in harmony with our new picture. We found a creative way of coming up with a down payment, and closing costs. The same month that we moved in to the new house, my husband started a different job that more than doubled his monthly income (another result of consciously applying the principles).

Our Father in Heaven helped us see that we are never stuck for good. We can elevate our thoughts, and elevate our life. We can free ourselves from bondage. We can change our circumstances. The power is within us; and it all begins with our thoughts. Plant good ideas in your mind, and do not pull them out. Let nature work its miracle. When God created the world, He did not have to force the creation. He said, "Let there be light." And there was light.

Nature is friendly to your plans, too. The formless substance wants form. Let it have form! The thing that keeps it from coming is your doubt, and your impatience with the seed. Give it time to grow. Leave it there long enough, until it has a chance to draw to itself the elements it needs.

So what *do* you want? If you knew you couldn't fail, what would your goals be? The sky's the limit, and as you hold tight to the laws as a kite to its string, you will soar. Dream big, because if you can think it, you can do it.

Now, are you ready for the bonus law? It's *finally* time to get into the Vacuum Law of Prosperity.

This one is amazing, because the results that come from abiding this law can be relatively quick...

THE VACUUM LAW OF PROSPERITY

This law was the one I consciously tried to apply first, because it was easy and just seemed to make a lot of sense to me. Seeing it work in a dramatic way, I was then given courage to test the rest of the laws which you have been studying in chapters 1-7. I list this principle last because it will be freshest in your memory when you finish the book, and it will be an excellent starting point for you to make some wonderful positive changes in your life.

Let me tell you about the circumstances surrounding the time when I first learned about and tested this law:

I met Bob Proctor for the first time during break at a seminar. After visiting for a minute, he told me that I had a pretty good balance going on between my right and my left brain (the creative and the analytical parts), but that I was primarily creative. I told him how I wasn't sure I believed him, because I had done my undergraduate studies in Mathematics. I felt *very* analytical, and I told him that I'm *always* analyzing, always hashing things out in my mind, and always *thinking*.

I wasn't sure, but his response sounded like an insult. He said, "You're NOT thinking. Your mind is busy, but you're not *thinking*."

Al-righty then! What do you say when a stranger tells you *that?* Well, I chewed on that for a while and almost a year later I finally figured out what he meant. By his definition, *thinking* meant creating a *new* thought, not rehashing or reorganizing old ones. To think is to consciously create a new idea limited only by one's imagination. It's thinking 'outside of the pie'; not focusing on limited visible resources.

For example, if I'm looking at my circumstances, and deducing whether or not my goal of prosperity is reasonable based on empirical evidence, then my mind is *busy analyzing*, but I'm not *thinking*. To dwell on circumstances as they are often leads to doubt and worry.

Instead, to *think* is to create a vision in my mind of how I want things to be, and then consciously choose to believe in the reality of my vision, *no matter the evidence...no matter what the circumstances are.* It is to live in the dream in my mind while acting upon those thoughts and patiently waiting for circumstances to eventually reflect them.

In my case, the checkbook said we were out of money, but I dreamed of having plenty. I literally spent time with my eyes closed, pretending that I already enjoyed the prosperity. I was *thinking*. If we manage to feel the emotions that would accompany the new lifestyle, then we are putting ourselves into a vibration that is in harmony with the things and circumstances we desire. When we *think*, our minds open up to the hidden ways that will make it happen.

When we only process evidence gathered by our five senses, our minds close up to the solutions to our problems. Our situation looks hopeless, because of the thoughts we choose. But in reality, our situation is never hopeless; we simply have to allow ourselves to *think,* and trust that the way will present itself.

So, what is the vacuum law? It goes like this: **Nature abhors a vacuum.** Let me explain:

Bob tells a story about his aunt. He paid her a visit, and she emphatically apologized for her hideous curtains. She expressed how much she hated those old curtains, but said she unfortunately couldn't afford to replace them.

Bob said, "You love those curtains."

"No, I hate them! I just can't *afford* to replace them."

"NO, you *love* them. Subconsciously you are in complete harmony with them, or they'd already be gone." Bob was blunt.

"But I can't *afford* new ones!" She explained.

"Dear Aunt, don't you see? You don't *need* new curtains; you have no place to hang any! If you want new curtains, take these down, clean them up, and give them away. Don't 'yard sale' them, donate them to charity."

After some time, he convinced her that since nature abhors a vacuum, it would not allow her to go long without the curtains she needs. But she would never get them so long as there were others already in their place. Hesitantly, Bob's aunt did as he said.

The next time he came to visit, there hung the new curtains. Somehow, a way had presented itself, and she was so amazed and inspired by the principle that now her living room was *void of furniture.*

When I heard that story, I thought, *here is a principle I can put to the test.* We had been apologizing for, and complaining about our carpet for three years. (Aside from *looking* bad, we remembered all too well what had been *on* it when be had bought the home as a 'repo'.) But since we had been going in the hole deeper by several hundred dollars every month, we couldn't justify replacing it. We came home from the seminar, immediately gave our kids some ketchup, honey, and markers...and told them to *go to town!* (The carpet was not even worth donating to a doghouse...) Then we pulled up the carpet, threw it out, and lived on concrete floors, dodging exposed tack strips for three weeks.

I did my homework, looking for the best deal on the kind of carpet we wanted, expecting that the way would present itself if I just kept moving my feet. Finally, after three weeks, the new carpet came. Somehow, we found a way without going into debt. I think it may have been an impound account overage on our home mortgage or another unexpected windfall which helped us fill the vacuum.

My friend did this for a couch. She gave away the older one, and was so excited to tell me about it when she got the new couch only a short time later. She afforded it with money which came and had been overlooked because it wasn't part of their regular income. There's a lesson in that: when we base our faith on evidence alone, we may even forget some of the more obvious avenues through which the money can come. If we think the goal is impossible based on only the most *obvious* evidence, then we can easily slip into discouragement and doubt, thus limiting the amount of blessings God can justify sending our way.

Maybe one way God leaves us to ourselves when we doubt and fear is by *not intervening* when our car is about to blow a head gasket. As a result, the unexpected money from the impound account gets used up for yet *another* frustrating repair bill. Maybe the *amount* of money coming your way isn't the variable factor every time, but whether or not you are spared an unexpected, unfortunate, and costly event. There are so many things we may never know...things that He does for us that we take for granted.

Take control of your life by setting some goals and controlling your thoughts. Once you decide where you want to go, He is *right there* and ready to help part the waters, so to speak, for YOU. However, with no goals and no direction, what intervention does a person need, anyway? That's like a drawbridge being lowered for a person when he or she has no intention of crossing to the other side. Set some goals!

Is applying the Vacuum Law an act of faith? Oh, yes it is. After all, what if the way *doesn't* present itself for the replacement carpet or new couch? This is when you practice believing anyway. Trust the laws and do *your* part. Your part is to believe and look for the way. Will your faith be strengthened when you practice having some? Most definitely. Like a muscle your faith is strengthened by exercising it. Our carpet experience gave us the courage to have faith in bigger dreams, which one by one, continue to come true. I am never surprised when they do, but always amazed.

We live in daily gratitude for the God-given blessings of abundance: the things that money can buy and the things that money *can't* buy. Above all, these principles have brought peace, and how can anyone put a price on *peace?* Live by the laws and you *will* live in peace.

I can't tell you where the money will come from for *you*. However, I *can* tell you a few of the sources from where it came for my husband and me during the lean years:

- A mechanical Santa was left on our doorstep anonymously with a one-hundred dollar bill in his hand.
- Our bank made an error resulting in a refund to our account.
- We received a larger than expected tax refund.
- I found a twenty dollar bill in my pocket that I never remembered having, at a time when a single dollar bill was tough to come by.
- We experienced a sudden increase in the number of customers/clients to our business.
- We found unbelievably good deals on major purchases like real estate, cars, computer equipment, etc.
- Some gift money arrived in the mail from a grandmother who had never given me money before, and who was, herself, as poor as a church mouse.
- And my favorite example: Four hundred dollars total came from the sale of four puppies out of my mutt who happened to mate with a loose, purebred Rhodesian Ridgeback. The puppies took on all the

distinguishing characteristics of the show-quality father. (Now, I *never* could have predicted that we could be saved financially that month by such a random blessing! Do you see how important it is to just *trust* in whatever the Lord will do, without knowing precisely *how* your deliverance will happen?)

THE CHALLENGE

I challenge you now to complete this section diligently. If you have internalized these ideas, you'll know it by the time you get done with this quiz. In reality, successfully applying these principles for the rest of your life is how you pass this test, but for sake of review, go ahead and give this section a try.

Keep this book and refer to it often. Teach someone else what you have learned. (You'll find a summary and a few more things at the end of the test.)

All about Laws

Name a *mushy* law and tell why it is mushy.

____

____

____

____

____

Explain the difference between obtaining wealth on the competitive plane and obtaining wealth on the creative plane.

____

____

____

Lesson 1 (Law of Perpetual Transmutation)

In your own words, state the definition of the Law of Perpetual Transmutation, and explain how it helps you obtain that which you seek.

____

____

____

____

All things are perpetually transmuting. With this in mind, list three things that once were a part of your life and are now gone. They can be any person, place, or thing.

____

____

____

____

Now list three things that you would like to see come into your life.

____

____

____

____

____

Lesson 2 (Law of Relativity)

In your own words, state the definition of the Law of Relativity and how it helps you maintain good thoughts. Tell why good thoughts are imperative.

____

____

____

____

In your opinion, what was the worst part of the pioneer's suffering?

____

____

____

____

What is the greatest challenge in your life right now?

____

____

____

____

Name three different ways that your challenge could actually be worse.

____

____

____

____

Lesson 3 (Law of Vibration)

In your own words, state the definition of the Law of Vibration and describe how it helps you attract what you desire.

____

____

____

____

____

Name 3 examples of modern communications that use vibrations to convey messages.

____

____

____

Name two examples of energy being transferred through vibrations in everyday life.

____

____

Name a particular location on this planet with a very low level of vibration.

____

Name a particular location on this planet with a very high level of vibration.

____

Name a person that you believe to be vibrating at a very high level...someone that seems to attract all the good they desire.

____

Study the scale on the next page. How would you identify the nature of your thinking most of the time? Where do spend most of your energy? The descriptive words intensify *and* accumulate as you approach the outer extremities.

------|------|------|------|------|------|------|------|------

fear bitterness doubt hope gratitude faith

Describe a new picture for your life.

____

____

____

____

____

____

____

Restate the Sea of Galilee principle.

____

____

____

____

____

In your own words, describe the *lesson* we learned from how an acorn becomes a great oak tree.

____

____

____

____

____

Lesson 4 (Law of Polarity)

In your own words, state the definition of the Law of Polarity and describe how it helps you think right during "bad" times.

____

____

____

____

Why wouldn't God want Gideon to have a very large army in the battle with the Midianites?

____

____

____

____

Which men were Gideon commanded to send home first?

Who were sent home next, and how many were left to fight?

Describe the ingenious strategy Gideon was directed by the Lord to use. How did they defeat the Midianites without even attacking them?

"Your desired results always follow a ______________________________"

Lesson 5 (Law of Rhythm)

In your own words, state the definition of the Law of Rhythm and describe how it helps you maintain hopeful thoughts.

Tell how keeping hopeful thoughts actually brings the upswing sooner.

What can we learn from a shoreline?

Honors student question: Think of something we have *not* discussed from nature that teaches a lesson about life. (Another example could be how most living things in the plant kingdom seem to reach for sunshine. From this we could learn that we should always seek greater light and knowledge from God.) What is still *another* lesson from nature?

Extend the car analogy to describe what could be happening to the car to represent a violation of one of God's laws. Include a description of the consequence for the violation.

What does it mean to become "past feeling," or desensitized, and how does it happen?

Lesson 6 (Law of Cause and Effect)

In your own words, state the definition of the Law of Cause and Effect.

For what purpose should we seek abundance?

Why should we seek to do good secretly, or without expectation of immediate reward?

Why should we be concerned with paying an honest tithe?

What is the acronym you should always remember for L.U.C.K.?

What is one thing you can do outside of business this week to make a difference like Joe, refusing payment for your casual service?

Lesson 7 (Law of Gender)

In your own words, state the two main ideas defined under the Law of Gender.

Name at least 3 idea-seed planters (good or bad) in your life.

In speeding up the process of taking an idea seed and growing it to maturity, what two factors are in your control?

How long will it take to get what you want?

Explain why we know it doesn't have to take twice as long to get twice as much.

Vacuum Law of Prosperity

Name one thing that you own which you despise. Tell why you've kept it so long.

Describe its replacement, if money were no object.

____
____
____
____
____
____
____

Do you have the courage to clean yours up and give it away; trusting that nature abhors a vacuum and the Lord will lead the way to help you get just what you want? ____________________________________

Conclusion

Once again, restate the new picture for your life.

____
____
____
____

Now, keep it securely planted, and have faith.

To help you remember these laws, there is a summary on the next page. Do whatever it takes to commit these new thought patterns to memory so that one day they will be instinctive. Practice, practice, practice! Even with every reason in the world to fear, we learn through practice how to "fear not." Just knowing why it is important to think faithfully helps me do it better. You will internalize these ideas best by teaching them, so now; who comes to mind that might be looking for some answers? Share them. It is my hope you will apply these principles and find greater peace, joy, fulfillment, and *prosperity*.

To your success,

Leslie Householder

SUMMARY

You cannot break a law;
You can only break yourself against it.

Law of Perpetual Transmutation—*Circumstances and things are perpetually coming or going according to your thoughts.*

Law of Relativity—*Your situation is not fundamentally good or bad until you compare it to something else.*

Law of Vibration—*Your thoughts control your personal vibration. Change your thoughts, get emotional about them, and you'll change what is attracted to you.*

Law of Polarity—*Everything has an opposite. A bad situation is equally good. Look for the good, and more good will be on its way.*

Law of Rhythm—*When you feel down be assured that an upswing is coming. Plan on endless progression upward.*

Law of Cause and Effect—*Action and reaction are equal, in opposite directions. Focus on what you can give, not what you will get.*

Law of Gender—*Plant your own idea seeds, and then be patient. Don't uproot your idea seed with doubt.*

Vacuum Law of Prosperity—*Nature abhors a vacuum. Make room for the thing you desire by giving away that which you do not like or use. Give it away, and let the Universe compensate you. God pays better than yard sale shoppers.*

INDEX

L

M

N

O

P

R

INDEX

W

ABOUT THE AUTHOR

Leslie Householder is a wife and mother of six young children. She is a seminar instructor, success coach, founder of ThoughtsAlive.com and the author of the modern-day adult allegory, "The Jackrabbit Factor: Why You Can." An earlier edition of Hidden Treasures has been sold as an ebook online under the title, "Heavenly Help with Money Matters" since 2002.

Leslie received her bachelor's degree from Brigham Young University in Mathematics Education. She loves the principles contained in this book because she has discovered they are as dependable as the sciences.

Presently serving as the Family Preparedness Specialist in her church, she has also served as a Humanitarian Aid Specialist, a teacher in the Young Women's organization, and a secretary and teacher in the Children's Primary Organization of her local congregation.

She's been a counselor for the Brigham Young University Academy for Girls, where she had her first opportunity to try her hand at motivational speaking more than a decade ago, (a dream she had since she was twelve). Since then, she has been a speaker at a number of venues including the SheLovesGod.com Annual Christian Women's conference and the Victor Valley Institute of Religion of Southern California. Her topics have included, "Working with your Subconscious mind to Achieve your Goals," "Leaning on the Lord in a Financial Crisis," and "Tuning in to the Abundance God has for You." She is a certified facilitator for numerous programs authored by Bob Proctor, including "Born Rich," "Principles of Prosperity (formerly called The Science of Getting Rich)," "The Goal Achiever," and "Mission in Commission." She has conducted live seminars in the continental U.S., and held numerous teleclasses servicing participants across the world.

Her articles have circulated online in numerous ezines internationally, and her writing has been included in a recent "Chicken Soup for the Soul" publication. Her goal-oriented articles have also been published in print magazines such as Opportunity World Magazine, Money N' Profits Magazine, and Career Source Magazine.

Her online newsletter at ThoughtsAlive.com services thousands of individuals who are striving to improve their thinking and their life. Her readers understand the value of positive input, and appreciate the brief, daily insights which help keep their thoughts uplifted. After all, it is by the small and simple things that great things are brought to pass.

ABOUT LESLIE'S OTHER BOOK

THE JACKRABBIT FACTOR: WHY YOU CAN

"[This story is] amazing! I'm near tears, on page [undisclosed]. This is hitting home. You have no idea how much I needed this, right this moment. Wow. Thank you. I'm writing down all that I know I will have. I have much to do, starting with being thankful to God for all my blessings." (Later...) "Okay, I'm in tears now! And feeling better and more positive, loved, guided and directed than I ever have in my entire life. I can't even begin to tell you how bad this day started, or the day before, but I know how it's going to end! Thank you so much for sharing [this story] with me. You are amazing! Just amazing. And you know what? So am I!" ~ ***Suzanne Staten, single mother.***

"I am genuinely impressed. Leslie has created a jewel in 'The Jackrabbit Factor.' It has been crafted such that a person can read and re-read it, and each time glean something new and empowering. In a unique and creative way, Leslie's story will lead her readers through successively increased levels of awareness and leave them not only with an

uncommon confidence, but more importantly, with the ability to make any life change they desire. Success-seekers of all degrees of knowledge and experience will benefit from this remarkable story. I strongly recommend you purchase multiple copies of this book for your family and friends." ~ ***Bob Proctor, founder Life Success Productions and best selling author of "You Were Born Rich"***

"I am actually at a loss for words after reading your manuscript. Kind of almost shook a little bit if that makes sense...The book was so well put together from a literary standpoint and the storyline was fantastic." ~ ***Fred Schofield, independent IT contractor.***

Introductory Summary of *The Jackrabbit Factor:*

The Goodmans have come to the end of their financial rope, and Felicity slips up, berating Richard for his failure to provide for the family. Defeated, Richard disappears into the woods behind their home and she fears he has gone to end his life. Guilt-ridden, she searches frantically, dealing with her own anxieties while trying to keep little Matthew unaware of the possible tragedy.

Richard has embarked on his own amazing and courageous journey where he discovers his own best advisor: his inner voice. Where has he gone, and what is required of Felicity before she is able to find him? Unlock with Richard the secret behind the voice of inspiration and find out for yourself how truly dependable and absolutely ingenious your own inner voice can be.

An excerpt from *The Jackrabbit Factor*:

Richard paused and cocked his head to one side. *A rabbit? It was chasing a rabbit this whole time!?* He chuckled out loud at his misconception. The dog had been chasing a rabbit. Suddenly it all made sense. The dog wasn't crazy, and it wasn't rabid. Richard recalled all of the jumping and growling, the darting to and fro… he laughed at himself for feeling anxious and making such a judgment.

"Oooooh, I'd like to have a rabbit, too…" Someone spoke from behind. Richard turned around, taken aback by the sudden company.

"Yeah, a rabbit would be nice. Much better than all those peanut butter sandwich, eh? M'name's Richard. What's yours?" Richard extended his hand to the small, round man now standing next to him with a five o'clock shadow and somewhat disheveled comb-over.

The man didn't break the stare he had fixed on the dog as it sauntered away, but politely replied, "Harold. Harold Ashway." He exhaled slowly and sighed, "I've gotta have one of those rabbits." His face lacked expression; he seemed awestruck by the sheer memory of the prize. Without another word, the man stepped off the road into the sheaves of grass and jogged clumsily ahead about forty feet. Then with a wave of his hand and a smile in Richard's direction, he turned and began to leap around as if he was chasing an elusive rabbit. Except…there was no rabbit.

Richard squinted. *What in the chickens is he doing...?*

Read this story. Experience the journey. Then watch amazing changes take place in your own life. You'll thank yourself for taking just one more step...

"I'm thoroughly impressed and inspired. In the same tradition as 'Richest Man in Babylon' and 'Who Moved My Cheese,' 'The Jackrabbit Factor' dives much deeper into how the mind works and how good things are attracted into our lives without

all the competition. I've studied a number of motivational/self-help books and programs to somehow figure out how to accomplish my goals. This book was insightful because it helped me realize that it is truly about ***my*** *dream and what motivates* ***me****. I can relax and know that as I cultivate my desires properly, all that I want is on its way; in fact, it is already here."* ~ ***Jeff Ackley, salesman, husband and father of five.***

"Well, I must say I'm amazed. You certainly have a knack for this. I guess I need to go write my goals down!" ~ ***Marcie Bringhurst, owner of windmill-designs.com and mother of six.***

"I was so happy to read your work with my family... I learned with them and in the process, knew that I was reading something inspiring. As I walked with Richard through the pages, I felt good knowing that wealthy, wise mentors do exist and want to share. I think that as a young adult I would have put this book up there with Jonathan Livingston Seagull--SOAR HIGH, BE AWARE, AND LIVE!" ~ ***Carolyn Tahauri, wife and mother of six.***

"Brilliant! Profound! Practical! Inspired and inspiring! Where were you, Leslie Householder, when I so desperately needed to read, 'The Jackrabbit Factor?' Your wonderful book is so

reminiscent of the spirit of 'Jonathan Livingston Seagull' and 'Illusions: The Adventures of A Reluctant Messiah' by Richard Bach. 'The Jackrabbit Factor' is destined to be a classic. Thank you, Leslie, for illuminating the world with the truth about how to live well. With my most sincere thanks and appreciation...congratulations!"
~Julian Kalmar, author of "Happiness: The Highest Gift." www.thehappinessformula.com

(Finally, comments from my own father…I couldn't resist including them here since they certainly put a smile on *my* face ☺)

"Leslie, I read your Jackrabbit Factor on the plane down today. Wow, I am totally impressed and quite embarrassed about my approach to all I do. Hey, all I gotta do is take LesterLessons and away we go! What I had read before was only a precursor to what you've created now, and the testimonials... will you remember me when you are on Oprah and raking in the big bucks? Just a few crumbs from your table.... I'm bursting with pride (is that bad?), think I'll just stand up and shout I KNOW LESLIE HOUSEHOLDER in my conference sessions this week. They might take me away, ha ha, but who cares! Give all them kinder a hug for me; sorry the conference isn't in Phoenix, maybe next year. Love, Pops"

ABOUT THE JACKRABBIT FACTOR

Quotes from James Allen's book are taken from *As a Man Thinketh,* New York: Peter Pauper Press, Inc.

Sign up for a free Insight of the Day at www.ThoughtsAlive.com to help you keep your thoughts where they need to be!

Watch a flash movie and read the first chapter of The Jackrabbit Factor at www.jackrabbitfactor.com

For more information, visit
www.ThoughtsAlive.com

For bulk order requests of either book, or to share your comments, send Leslie a message through www.thoughtsalive.com or write:

Leslie Householder
THOUGHTSALIVE
P.O. Box 31749
Mesa, AZ 85275